SCHOOL OF AMERICAN RESEARCH

GRAND CANYON
ARCHAEOLOGICAL SERIES

The publication of this volume
was made possible by a grant from the
DONALD B. ANDERSON FOUNDATION

ARCHAEOLOGY OF THE GRAND CANYON:
THE WALHALLA PLATEAU

Douglas W. Schwartz
Jane Kepp
Richard C. Chapman

School of American Research Press
Grand Canyon Archaeological Series, Volume 3

SCHOOL OF AMERICAN RESEARCH PRESS
Post Office Box 2188
Santa Fe, New Mexico 87501

Contents

MAPS AND FIGURES

Contents

Contents

TABLES

Preface

To stand on the North Rim of the Grand Canyon is to be faced with one of the most startling contrasts in nature. Spreading away to the south are the dry reds and browns, the rugged shapes, and the vast panoramas of the canyon, while at one's back are the cool greens and gentle, shaded slopes of the forested plateau. The contrast of color, depth, and terrain is so extraordinary that the viewer is constrained to pause and try to capture the essence of one of the world's more awesome natural regions.

The luxuriant forests covering hundreds of square miles north of the Grand Canyon have a primal quality, which can transport a traveler into some forgotten past. On the high plateau, one can walk for miles without seeing another human being, hearing only the occasional raucous cry of a Steller's jay or the chattering of a Kaibab squirrel. Venturing toward the edge of the plateau, the traveler chances upon unexpected vistas where the land drops away precipitously to reveal the magnificence of the Grand Canyon.

From its brink, the canyon appears uncompromisingly inaccessible, with its massive cliff faces and overpowering depths and distances. Unlike the peaceful forests of the plateau, the canyon gives the impression of being at war with humans, challenging the survival of any who might invade. One feels instantly that the canyon is an absolute barrier, impossible to cross, founded upon a raging river that must always have separated distinct worlds on either side.

These were some of the impressions that were imprinted on my mind when I first visited the Grand Canyon in the late 1940s. Firmly but unconsciously, my first perceptions began to influence my thinking as I explored for evidence of prehistoric people. Scattered across the plateaus and throughout the canyon were an assortment of petroglyphs, masonry outlines of pueblos, clusters of pottery and stone tools, and cliff granaries, all attesting to the presence of Anasazi people centuries earlier.

It did not surprise me that the pleasant, nonthreatening plateaus stretching away from the canyon rim had supported prehistoric populations. But the discovery that the canyon itself held prehistoric ruins came as an intriguing revelation, for to me it seemed improbable that this inhospitable gorge could have supported aboriginal life. I became fascinated by the canyon and its human past, and as I look back 30 years to my initial observations and questions, I realize that I unconsciously formulated several assumptions about the prehistory of the Grand Canyon region.

I assumed that the beautiful North Rim country and, to a lesser degree, the plateau south of the canyon were the more desirable locations for prehistoric farmers. Therefore, these areas would naturally have been the first and most continuously inhabited. In contrast, I believed that settlement of the canyon must have been undertaken only under extreme necessity. Finally, I saw the Colorado River as a powerful barrier to human passage, effectively dividing the canyon country into two distinct spheres of cultural development.

These implicit assumptions influenced the design of several archaeological surveys that I conducted throughout the Grand Canyon during the next 15 years. However, as I gathered more information, a picture of Grand Canyon prehistory began to emerge that was substantially at odds with the original assumptions. Gradually I realized that the North Rim had not been the hub of prehistoric settlement, that the canyon actually had much to offer to early subsistence farmers, and that the river had not always been a barrier to travel and communication.

Equipped with these evolving ideas, I developed a program of three excavation projects to focus on specific questions of chronology, subsistence economy, and the relationship of the prehistoric inhabitants to their environment. The first project took place at Unkar Delta, a broad outwash at the confluence of Unkar Creek and the Colorado River, which had been the site of a relatively large prehistoric community

(Schwartz, Chapman, and Kepp 1980). A second project was the excavation of a small, isolated pueblo downstream from Unkar Delta at the mouth of Bright Angel Creek (Schwartz, Marshall, and Kepp 1979). The third project, centering on a portion of the plateau north of the Grand Canyon known as the Walhalla Glades, is the subject of this book.

From the beginning of the excavation program, I planned to publish the results of each project separately in three largely descriptive monographs. Therefore, the present volume explores little of the relationship between the prehistoric people of the Walhalla Plateau and those of the rest of the Grand Canyon region. Such broader issues will be taken up in the final volume of this series, a synthesis of the data from all the projects that will place each area of excavation in its context within the prehistory of the larger region. In addition, the final book will return to the questions that originally stimulated the research program, including the dynamics of settlement expansion and the nature of cultural success and failure in marginal environments.

With the publication of this monograph, all my Grand Canyon fieldwork of the past 30 years is documented. In reviewing the projects, especially the excavations begun more than a decade ago, I can see that I might have approached some aspects of the work differently and can think of many other questions I might profitably have asked. But no ideal culmination of data collection can ever be reached; at some point the fieldwork and analysis must stop and the current interpretations be reported. Taking a historical view of research, I assume that future studies will alter and elaborate upon the conclusions presented here, especially because the Grand Canyon received so little archaeological attention until recent years.

My work in the Grand Canyon led me down many fascinating trails, both on the ground and of the intellect. It was a part of my professional and personal life that I would not trade for any other episode. I cannot help wondering whether an archaeological project of the kind described here can truly be understood in detachment from the many events and adventures that have made fieldwork in the Grand Canyon, for me, so personally enriching an experience.

Douglas W. Schwartz

Acknowledgments

The Walhalla Plateau archaeological project was made possible by grants from the National Geographic Society, the National Park Service, and the Grand Canyon Natural History Association. Additional support from the National Park Service allowed us to complete the data analysis and prepare this volume for publication.

The field crews contributed to the success of the project through their hard work and sustained good humor. They included the following people: Mike Chapel and Reba Ferguson, cooks; Don Dix and Rick Miranda, camp supervisors; Karl Kernberger and Jerry Wiley, photographers; Richard C. Chapman, field supervisor; crew chiefs John D. Beal, Edward Crocker, Gene Paull, Theodore Reinhart, Ed Sudderth, and Jack Woolley; excavators Bill Adams, Selvin Banner, Christopher Causey, Robert Costales, John Dessauer, Jay Dillon, Steve Fleegle, Mike Hancock, Laurance Linford, Charles Padilla, Jerry Robinson, Susan Schwartz, Steven Schwartz, Greg Stark, and Tom Zanic. Laboratory personnel included Patricia Hanrahan, Deborah Pratt, John Rawlins, Mike Stanford, and Rosina Thornburg.

The project ecologists, whose work contributed much to the contents of Chapter 2, were Gerald Thornton in 1969 and Karen Lundquist and Harold Stacy in 1970. Others who provided information for Chapter 2 were Peter S. Bennett, who analyzed pollen samples for cultigen pollen; Hugh C. Cutler and Leonard Blake, who examined the plant remains; and Arthur H. Harris, who identified the faunal remains.

We would also like to thank Peter Eidenbach for his thorough analysis of the human skeletal material, Michael P. Marshall for classifying the ceramics, and Theodore Reinhart for his study of the ground stone artifacts recovered during the 1969 field season.

Special thanks are extended to several individuals who helped in a variety of ways. Harvey Butchart generously shared with us his knowledge of the Grand Canyon and its prehistoric ruins and trails. David Ochsner, of Grand Canyon National Park, did much to ease us through logistics problems, and Douglas Scovill, chief archaeologist for the National Park Service, maintained patience through the long preparation and publication of this volume. John D. Beal's memory and intellectual support have filled many gaps in our field notes and aided in interpreting the findings of the project.

The maps and diagrams in this book were drawn by Lynne Arany, the site plans by Rachel Conine. David G. Noble photographed the artifacts. The fine work of these three is greatly appreciated. We thank Richard W. Effland, Jr., and Gary Matlock for their helpful reviews of an earlier draft of the manuscript. Finally, we are grateful for the generous support of the Donald B. Anderson Foundation, which made possible the publication of this volume.

1

Introduction

During 1969 and 1970, the School of American Research conducted archaeological investigations on the North Rim of the Grand Canyon. This work was part of a four-year, three-phase research program of which the broad objective was to reconstruct the culture history of the Grand Canyon and the immediately surrounding region. Specifically, the research focused on five main topics: (1) the chronological and cultural sequence of prehistoric events, (2) the reasons for settlement and abandonment of the various ecological settings in the region, (3) the nature of cultural adaptation to the quite different environments of the canyon and plateau, (4) the cultural consequences of movement into new and different localities, and (5) the cultural characteristics of people living on the margins of Anasazi distribution. These topics were to be examined through a program of survey, excavation, and ecological study in several contrasting locations that had not previously been explored with intensive archaeological research.

The first phase of the project took place in 1967 and 1968 on Unkar Delta, a 50-hectare outwash at the confluence of Unkar Creek and the Colorado River. Excavation at 31 sites revealed many details about life in a relatively large, prehistoric canyon settlement (Schwartz, Chapman, and Kepp 1980). The second phase of the research was the excavation in 1969 of a small, isolated pueblo located downstream from Unkar Delta at the mouth of Bright Angel Creek in the narrow Granite Gorge (Schwartz, Marshall, and Kepp 1979). Finally, this

1

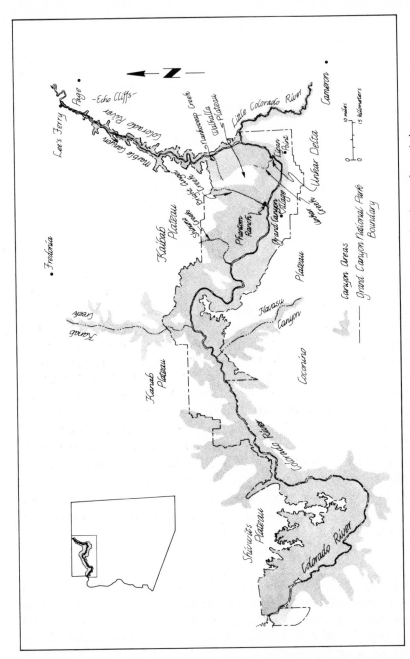

MAP 1. Grand Canyon National Park and surrounding region in northern Arizona.

2

volume reports on the third phase of the project, which was carried out in 1969 and 1970 on the high, forested Walhalla Plateau north of the Grand Canyon (Map 1).

The first written record of Native Americans living just north of the Grand Canyon was made in 1776 by Fray Silvestre Escalante. Traveling through the area in an unsuccessful attempt to find a route from Santa Fe, New Mexico, to California, Escalante met a group of Paiutes who told him of their hunting-and-gathering way of life (Auerbach 1943:90–92). Paiutes were still using the North Rim seasonally during the late nineteenth and early twentieth centuries but then began to consolidate to the north along the Utah border, especially at the Pipe Springs reservation. In the early 1900s, the first archaeological reports about the North Rim were published (James 1900; Judd 1926; West 1923). The writers generally agreed that "these ancient Pueblos and cliff dwellings were in ages past occupied by the ancestors of the present Pueblo tribes" (West 1923:74).

Not until the late 1930s was the first systematic archaeological work carried out on the North Rim. Edward T. Hall, Jr., conducted an inventory survey of a portion of the Walhalla Plateau called the Walhalla Glades (Hall 1942), recording 273 sites, including single, masonry rooms, multiroom pueblos, agricultural terraces, and check dams. From an analysis of ceramics collected at these sites, Hall hypothesized a prehistoric sequence of occupation by Anasazi people that lasted from A.D. 700 to 1200, with a population peak between about A.D. 900 and 1100 and then a rapid decline.

The School of American Research also chose the Walhalla Glades as an accessible, environmentally varied, conveniently sized study area that would allow controlled survey and excavation. The Glades are a "peninsula" of land that extends southward from the main portion of the Walhalla Plateau, to which they are joined by a narrow bridge of land (Map 2; Fig. 1). Surrounded on three sides by the canyons of drainages tributary to the Colorado River—Clear Creek, Unkar Creek, Lava Creek, and others—the Glades must have been served by many access routes from the canyon bottom. Therefore, we believed that the Glades would provide data suitable for eventual comparison with data from Unkar Delta and other canyon settlements. Finally, our choice of the Walhalla Glades was influenced by the availability of information from Hall's earlier survey, which we saw as a solid foundation on which our work could build.

3

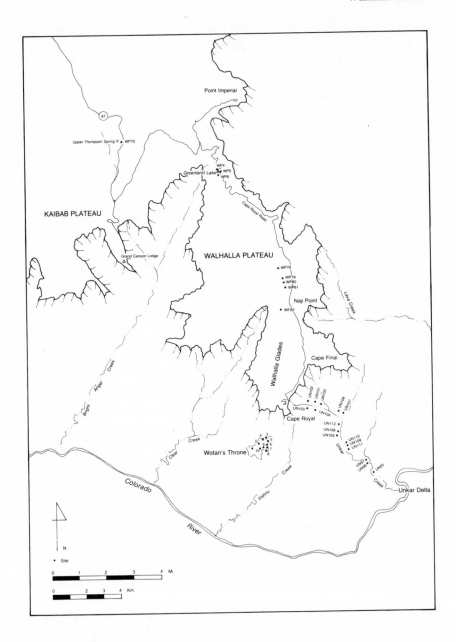

MAP 2. The Walhalla Glades and surroundings, showing locations of sites outside the main study area.

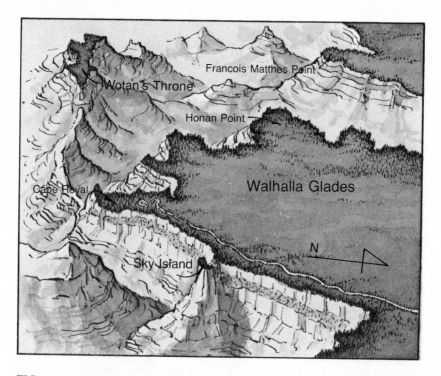

FIG. 1. Topography of the Walhalla Glades (drawing by the late Robert Nicholson).

The primary objectives of the North Rim project were (1) to analyze the ecology of the Walhalla Glades in order to obtain a data base for reconstructing the prehistoric environment and past economic adaptations, (2) to survey the Glades and adjacent areas in order to determine the sequence of prehistoric occupation, (3) by excavating, to obtain information about cultural adaptation and change throughout the occupation sequence, (4) to investigate the factors that influenced the observed cultural changes, (5) to examine the timing and nature of the abandonment of the area, and (6) to gather additional data to refine further our growing understanding of Grand Canyon prehistory.

To accomplish these objectives, surveys were conducted that crosscut all the vegetation zones of the Glades and sampled several locations outside the immediate study area. Of the 94 sites recorded, 25 were chosen for testing or complete excavation on the basis of date, location, and configuration. The results of this work revealed a use of the Walhalla Plateau by hunting bands between about 100 B.C. and

A.D. 500, separated by an apparent hiatus from a sequence of settlement by farming people between about A.D. 1050 and 1150.

SETTLEMENT HISTORY

Characteristic Basketmaker II projectile points were found near a small sinkhole known as Greenland Lake, north of the main study area (Map 2), indicating that small hunting parties had established temporary camps there sometime between 100 B.C. and A.D. 500. The resources of the plateau might well have attracted similar bands as much as 2,000 years earlier, when hunters left evidence of their forays into the Grand Canyon itself; but no direct evidence to support this hypothesis was found during the North Rim project.

The first Pueblo use of the Glades began about A.D. 950 or perhaps somewhat later. Evidence for human habitation at that time is scant, no more than some potsherds characteristic of the late Pueblo I and early Pueblo II periods. We assume that the people who left this pottery were seasonal farmers, as their successors were. Given the cool temperatures and short growing season of the high plateau, it is understandable that the earliest Pueblo use of the Glades was tentative and sporadic. In fact, the mere presence of farming people in this marginal environment suggests that substantial pressure for arable land must already have been felt on the Colorado Plateau.

It was not until about A.D. 1050 that population began to increase rapidly, if the large number of sites found across the Walhalla Glades is any reflection of population size. Most sites dating between A.D. 1050 and 1100 were quite small, consisting only of one or two rooms that apparently served as temporary dwellings and storage facilities for people who came to the plateau during the summers to farm. The stone outlines of rooms dotted the landscape all the way to the 2,500-meter elevation line, making the Glades one of the highest areas in the Southwest to support a farming population. The residents also built extensive systems of artificial agricultural terraces on gently sloping ridgetops and upper hillsides where erosion could be controlled. With the long, harsh winters of the plateau and the proximity of lower, warmer areas, it is not surprising that the occupation of the Walhalla Glades appears to have been a seasonal one.

Sometime before A.D. 1100, the number of people using the plateau apparently began to dwindle, and fewer sites were constructed after that time. Most of the sites occupied the same kinds of locations as had those of the preceding years, that is, the tops or upper slopes of the broad ridges bordering the drainages. Average site size increased slightly, chiefly because the one-room structures that had formerly been so abundant were no longer constructed. Most sites now consisted of two or three rooms, with an occasional pueblo having as many as eighteen rooms. A few sites appeared in new, spectacular locations on rock pillars standing away from the rim of the plateau, specifically two known as Sky Island and Wotan's Throne. These locations served as storage and collection stations and perhaps were used also for limited farming and habitation. The difficulty of access to these pillars speaks of a degree of stress in the lives of the North Rim inhabitants at this time and adds a rather dramatic note to the culture history of the area.

In the early years of the twelfth century, the climate of the northern Southwest began to deteriorate, and by about A.D. 1140, drought was severe. This change was disastrous for people farming in a marginal location such as the Walhalla Plateau. Eventually, agriculture became impossible on the North Rim, and by at least A.D. 1150, the plateau was abandoned along with most areas of Pueblo settlement in the Grand Canyon region.

RESEARCH DESIGN

The research design for the Walhalla Plateau project included three major areas of fieldwork and subsequent analysis: site survey, excavation, and ecological study. During the 1969 field season, the main objective was to gather a broad spectrum of information that would provide an overview of site distribution and chronology. It was then possible during the following summer to focus the research strategy on work necessary to answer questions raised by analysis of data from the first season.

Survey

Both to check and to supplement Hall's 1939 survey records, the School of American Research (SAR) began its 1969 field season with surveys of three areas of the Walhalla Glades (Map 3). These areas

7

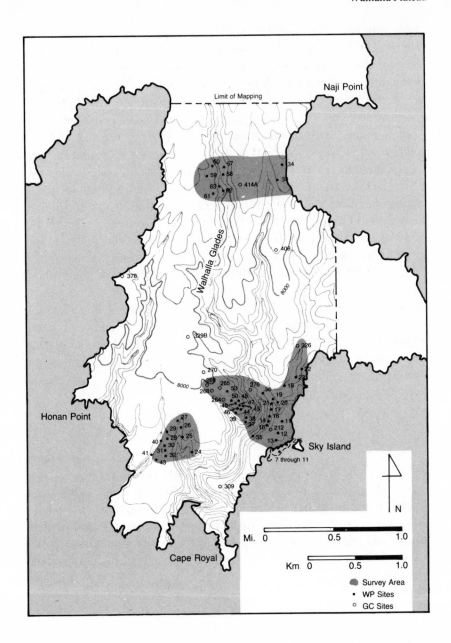

MAP 3. Locations of SAR survey areas, WP sites, and GC sites relocated in 1969–70.

were selected because they encompassed much of the range of geographic, topographic, and vegetative variability in the Glades. Acces-
sibility from the only paved road in the Glades also influenced the
choice of survey areas. A four-person crew first walked the areas and
flagged all definite or possible sites. For purposes of the project, a site
was defined as any noticeable human alteration of the natural environment and thus could encompass everything from isolated stone implements to multiroom pueblos. After this initial locating of the sites, a
two-person crew went back over the areas, recording each site and
collecting all artifacts that could be found on the site surface. Numerical site designations prefixed with "WP" (Walhalla Plateau) were
assigned to the recorded sites. Efforts were then made to identify sites
previously described by Hall, and when such identification could be
made, the original "GC" (Grand Canyon) numbers were adopted.
Most sites, however, could not be correlated with certainty with Hall's
records. Some of the sites undoubtedly were newly discovered, but
others probably duplicated Hall's findings.

In general, the results of the SAR survey corresponded well with
Hall's records. A somewhat larger number of sites was recorded, but
this discrepancy arose mainly because the SAR survey assigned site
numbers to all types of features, including sherd and lithic scatters and
agricultural terraces, whereas Hall had described such features but
gave numbers chiefly to habitation sites.

During the 1970 field season, three smaller surveys were undertaken
for specific reasons. First, both the previous year's survey and Hall's
data indicated that site density and site size tended to decrease toward
the higher elevations in the northern part of the Walhalla Glades,
where ponderosa pine begins to give way to fir. A relatively informal
check was made of an area at and just above the 2,500-meter (8,200-
foot) contour line. The five sites located tended to bear out the earlier
observation, four of the sites consisting of low rubble mounds probably representing a single room each, and the fifth, situated at about
2,536 meters, being a sherd scatter. Spot checks of several locations
much farther north, beyond the Walhalla Glades, yielded a few lithic
sites around Greenland Lake and one near Upper Thompson Spring on
the Kaibab Plateau (Map 2), but no structures.

One of the larger sites discovered by Hall that was relocated in
1969, GC215, was situated on a rock pillar known as Sky Island,
isolated but accessible from the rim of the plateau (Fig. 2). To ascer-

FIG. 2. View of Sky Island from the north.

tain whether this site was a unique occurrence or whether other rock pillars were also occupied, a larger one called Wotan's Throne (Map 2) was surveyed in 1970. Wotan's Throne lies about 2 km southwest of Cape Royal, is roughly 40 ha (100 acres) on the top, and is accessible both from the canyon bottom and, with somewhat greater difficulty, from the North Rim. A crew of four was transported to Wotan's Throne by helicopter and, in surveying the area, located ten sites. These ranged from a cluster of sherds belonging to a single vessel to several small, crude, masonry rooms. The results of the survey suggested that prehistoric use of these seemingly unusual locations might not have been a rare occurrence.

The third 1970 survey area was the canyon of Unkar Creek, which leads from the east side of the Walhalla Glades to the Colorado River about 9 km away (Fig. 3). Four sites had previously been found in the lower part of Unkar Canyon during the 1967–68 project on Unkar Delta. To determine whether site distribution was continuous all the way to the North Rim, a team walked the length of the canyon in 1970, locating twelve additional sites. Of the total, at least six and possibly

FIG. 3. View from the southeast edge of the Walhalla Glades down Unkar Creek to the Colorado River.

eight sites appeared to be habitations, four were small granaries situated in overhangs in the cliffs, three were lithic scatters, and one was an isolated hearth. All these sites have been described in an earlier publication (Schwartz, Chapman, and Kepp 1980).

All the surveys just described, excluding the reconnaissance of Unkar Canyon, yielded records on a total of 94 sites (see Table 4). Of these, 14 were originally discovered by Hall in 1939 and relocated by SAR, while the remainder either were found for the first time by SAR or could not be correlated definitely with Hall's descriptions. Actually, many more of Hall's sites were relocated but not redescribed by SAR, and many features such as fallen rooms and agricultural terraces were noticed outside the SAR survey areas but were not recorded or given site numbers.

More than half the sites (58.5 percent) were structures or probable structures ranging from single, masonry rooms to groups of roomblocks containing 18 rooms or possibly more. Among the probable habitation/ storage sites, small units of one or two rooms predominated (73 per-

11

cent). Agricultural terraces and check dams made up 12 percent of the total, sherd and lithic scatters another 12 percent, and the remainder included pictographs, rock-shelters, granaries, and features that could not be clearly identified.

Site density was heavy in the two southernmost areas surveyed by SAR, less so in the northernmost area (Map 3). With Hall's data added to our own, it is obvious that sites are scattered over the entire Walhalla Glades, with densities greatest along the edges of ridges overlooking drainage valleys rather than on the broad, flat areas between drainages (Map 4). Toward the 2,500-meter contour line, in transitional ponderosa pine–fir forest, sites thin out and are virtually unknown above that elevation. The number of sites known from the Walhalla Glades leaves no doubt that the area was heavily occupied by prehistoric people.

Excavation

Following the 1969 survey, Michael P. Marshall classified the ceramic collection to allow preliminary dating of the sites. Earlier, Marshall had reexamined Hall's 1939 collections so that many sites not relocated by SAR could also be tentatively dated. The datable sites were classified as either Pueblo I (A.D. 850–950), Pueblo II (950–1100), or Pueblo III (1100–1150). Because the goals of the project demanded sizable artifact collections and data on site configurations that could not be obtained through survey alone, it was decided to test or excavate as many sites as possible for each time period. Undated sites including habitations, agricultural terraces, lithic concentrations, and rock-shelters were also included in the testing program.

During 1969, the most intensive work took place at the relatively large site GC212/212A, which was almost completely excavated. In addition, a crew cleared rooms or test trenches at one presumed Pueblo I site, ten Pueblo II sites, three Pueblo III sites, two lithic sites, two agricultural terraces, and four undated sites.

In 1970, four sites were chosen for complete or extensive excavation. These were WP5, a lithic concentration near Greenland Lake, north of the Walhalla Glades; GC378, a single room tentatively dated to the Pueblo I period; GC408, a two-room structure belonging to the Pueblo II interval; and GC215, a large Pueblo III site located on the rock pinnacle, Sky Island. WP5, GC408, and GC215 had been tested

12

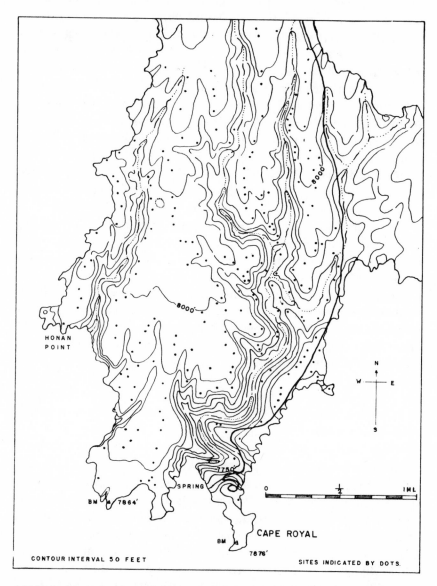

MAP 4. Reproduction of map published by Edward T. Hall, Jr. (1942), showing sites located during his survey of the Walhalla Glades (courtesy of Museum of Northern Arizona Press).

in 1969 and yielded considerable amounts of cultural material and, in the last two cases, well-preserved architectural features. Another small site, KP1, located near the Grand Canyon Lodge on the Kaibab Plateau, was excavated at the request of the National Park Service for use in its interpretive program.

As a result of the testing and excavation, 14 sites were completely or extensively cleared, and 11 were subjected to more limited testing. Analysis of pottery collected during excavation made possible the refinement of the initial, tentative chronological framework. Sometimes the date previously assigned to a site on the basis of survey samples had to be altered when larger excavation samples became available. In the end, sites that could be dated were assigned to one of three time periods: A.D. 950–1050, 1050–1100, and 1100–1150.

Among the sites with habitation or storage rooms or both, masonry construction was virtually universal, although in many cases only one or a few courses remained of the walls. Both interior and exterior features such as fire pits, cists, and bins were rare, and site configuration in general was fairly uniform, even across time periods. Agricultural terraces were found to consist of low, drylaid, stone alignments running parallel to the contours of hills and holding back as much as 25 cm of soil. A summary of the excavation results is presented in Chapter 4, and detailed descriptions of all the sites can be found in Appendix A.

Ecological Studies

The archaeological surveys and excavations in the Walhalla Glades were accompanied by several ecological studies intended to aid in interpreting the prehistoric economic adaptation to the plateau environment. In 1969, Gerald Thornton began compiling basic information about the geology, climate, vegetation, fauna, and other aspects of the Glades and surrounding area, with special emphasis on identifying edible wild plants that might have been used by the prehistoric inhabitants. Thornton also planted a group of experimental gardens to determine whether crops could be raised with no other water than rainfall. The experimental garden project was continued in 1970 by Harold Stacy and Karen Lundquist, who also compiled a vegetation map of the Walhalla Glades and conducted studies of vegetation in the ponderosa pine forest, the pine-fir transition zone, and the piñon-juniper wood-land.

Together these studies provided a basic understanding of the economic potential of the Walhalla Glades for the Anasazi who once lived there. While the plateau and adjacent canyon slopes offer abundant plant and animal resources and raw materials for building and tools, the Walhalla Glades seem only marginally suitable for agriculture at present. The growing season is short, and the spring drought demands that gardens be watered artificially for two or three weeks after planting. Nevertheless, we have good evidence in the form of plant remains, cultigen pollen, and agricultural terraces that prehistoric farming was successful for some time on the plateau. The feasibility of agriculture in the Walhalla Glades is a crucial issue in interpreting the prehistory of the area.

2

The Physical Environment

The Walhalla Glades cover a relatively low plateau ranging in elevation from 2,393 meters (7,850 feet) above sea level at Cape Royal on the south to about 2,500 meters (8,200 feet) where the Glades join the main body of the Walhalla Plateau. On the west, the Glades fall away precipitously to the canyon of Clear Creek, while on the east the same steep cliffs prevail but lead to a more broken, gradually stepped terrain with numerous saddles, buttes, and pinnacles. To the north, the adjacent Walhalla Plateau stands even higher, reaching about 2,590 meters (8,500 feet) near Greenland Lake. This land mass in turn adjoins the Kaibab Plateau, a huge block fault rising as high as 2,804 meters (9,200 feet) and sloping away to the east and west.

With their lower elevation, the Walhalla Glades support mostly ponderosa pine forest, in contrast to the fir, spruce, and mountain meadow plant communities found on the higher plateaus to the north. The climate is also milder than that of the higher elevations but still is generally cool and moist, with an average annual temperature of 7 degrees Celsius (45 degrees F.) and average yearly precipitation of 61 cm (24 in.). Today, the mule deer is the predominant mammal of the Walhalla Glades, and it was probably an important food resource prehistorically.

GEOLOGY AND TOPOGRAPHY

The many, layered rock formations that make up the Walhalla Plateau are, like those of the larger Kaibab Plateau, capped by the Kaibab formation, a stratum consisting of sandy limestone, calcareous sandstone, and bedded chert (Brown 1969:171). The rock of this formation is friable and breaks naturally into tabular pieces at outcroppings, thus providing a readily available building material. Its extensive inclusions of chert offer a prime source of raw material for stone tools.

Although the limestone itself is quite porous, it weathers into clay at the ground surface. Layers of such clay up to 1.5 m thick were observed in places in the Walhalla Glades, and most excavated architectural features were found to be resting directly on this stratum. These impermeable clays probably account for the precipitation runoff that has dissected the Glades with several shallow but steep-sided drainage valleys. Trending from north to south, these valleys are a maximum of 90–120 meters (300–400 feet) deep in local relief and are separated by fairly broad, level ridges. Occasionally the erosion channels contain water for a short time after heavy thunderstorms or during spring snowmelt.

Despite the presence of the drainage valleys, there is no permanent standing water in the Walhalla Glades today. The nearest such water source is Greenland Lake (Fig. 4), 11 km north of the central portion of the Glades. Actually a small sinkhole, this "lake" usually contains water year-round, though the supply diminishes during the summer. During the crucial spring planting time, it certainly would have held water from winter snows. Perhaps the major sources of water for prehistoric people in the Walhalla Glades were springs and seeps located around the perimeter of the plateau below the rim, though these are few and sometimes difficult to reach. Probably of greatest importance to the Glades was Cliff Spring, located on the west side of Cape Royal. Grand Canyon National Park records of flow measurements from Cliff Spring show quantities ranging from 26 to 216 liters (7 to 57 gallons) per hour on seven occasions from 1937 to 1940, in the months of June–September, with an average of 76 liters per hour. Just below the east rim of the Glades, in the vicinity of a group of pictographs designated as WP7 through WP11, were a number of seeps emerging from the cliff face, and several small seeps were also noticed in the erosional channels on the top of the plateau. At times when precipitation was greater than it is today, water from such seeps might have

18

FIG. 4. Greenland Lake.

been more abundant. Still, water for daily use may never have been plentiful in the Walhalla Glades.

Soils on the plateau are typically thin, acid forest soils, usually rocky and dull grayish brown in color. Two soil samples from site GC212 were tested for pH, with results of 5.5 (acid) for a sample taken from the ground surface and 6.0 (slightly acid) for a clay sample taken 30 cm below surface. Although only two samples were tested, the findings probably are generally applicable to soils across the Walhalla Glades as a whole. Much of the surface of the Glades is covered by a few centimeters of pine duff, and outcrops of limestone are common. As mentioned earlier, a layer of dense red clay underlying the soil appears to be extensive.

CLIMATE

The climate of the Walhalla Glades is conditioned by the elevation, the position of the Glades relative to the Grand Canyon, and their southern exposure. The elevation produces cool summers, cold winters, and moderately heavy precipitation. However, the Glades are almost entirely south exposed and are surrounded on three sides by the Grand Canyon, from which rise updrafts of warm air. These two factors probably act to make winter temperatures somewhat less severe than those of the Kaibab Plateau, and perhaps they prevent extreme accumulations of snow and lengthen the growing season slightly.

No weather records have ever been kept in the Walhalla Glades, but some are available from the Bright Angel Ranger Station 11 km to the northwest. Because the station is situated at an elevation of about 2,560 meters, the precipitation recorded there is probably somewhat too high for the Glades and the temperature data slightly too low, but they do provide a reasonable approximation. The records are not complete because in many years, especially since 1960, the station has not been kept open in the winter.

However, complete precipitation data were recorded during 22 years between 1930 and 1957. Mean annual precipitation for those years was 62.28 cm (24.52 in.), with a range from 35 cm (13.92 in.) to 93 cm (36.75 in.). The greatest amount of precipitation fell as snow during the months of December through March (Table 1), and summer thunderstorms accounted for fairly heavy rainfall during July through September. The spring months of April through June were usually the driest. Average annual snow accumulation on the Kaibab Plateau is more than 381 cm (150 in.) (Sellers 1960) but probably is somewhat less in the Walhalla Glades.

Mean annual temperature at the Bright Angel Ranger Station is 6 degrees C (43 degrees F.), with a January average of −3 degrees C (26 degrees F.) and a July average of 16 degrees C (62 degrees F.) (Sellers 1960). The frost-free period averages 101 days (Sellers 1960) between mid-June and mid-September. For reasons already mentioned, we estimate that the growing season is slightly longer in the Walhalla Glades, but it probably is still barely adequate at present for the successful raising of corn, beans, or squash.

VEGETATION

Virtually the only biotic community present in the Walhalla Glades today is the ponderosa pine *(Pinus ponderosa)* forest (Map 5). A narrow belt of piñon-juniper *(Pinus edulis, Juniperus osteosperma)* woodland is found at the southern tip of the plateau, as are several

20

TABLE 1.
Monthly precipitation on the Kaibab Plateau,
1930–31, 1933–36, 1938–42, and 1947–57.
Records from Bright Angel Ranger Station.

	Mean (inches)	Lowest Recorded	Highest Recorded
January	3.39	0.63	7.73
February	2.74	0.62	5.40
March	2.68	0.00	7.88
April	1.43	0.08	6.16
May	1.22	0.07	4.67
June	0.98	0.00	3.15
July	1.83	0.17	3.25
August	2.90	0.39	8.34
September	1.96	0.00	12.31
October	1.26	0.00	4.10
November	1.50	0.00	4.70
December	2.77	0.00	8.84

NOTE: Measurements are given in inches as originally recorded before conversion to the metric system.

areas covered with sagebrush *(Artemisia tridentata)* (Fig. 5). Elsewhere, ponderosa pine occurs either in nearly pure stands or intermixed with lesser amounts of other species: aspen *(Populus tremuloides)* on the cooler slopes of the northern part of the Glades; white fir *(Abies concolor)* and Douglas fir *(Pseudotsuga taxifolia)* along the western rim; and Gambel oak *(Quercus gambelii)* along the major drainage in the southeastern portion of the plateau.

Both the shade produced by the ponderosa canopy and the heavy duff or needle litter from the trees effectively inhibit the development of understory vegetation. Consequently the forest is very open, with broad, clear spaces between trees supporting only a few grasses, forbs, and shrubs (Fig. 6). The predominant understory grasses are Arizona fescue *(Festuca arizonica),* mountain muhly *(Muhlenbergia montana),* squirreltail *(Sitanion hystrix),* and June grass *(Koeleria cristata).* The most abundant forbs include species of lupine *(Lupinus* sp.), wild buckwheat *(Eriogonum* sp.), gold-aster *(Chrysopsis* sp.), pussytoes *(Antennaria* sp.), and catchfly *(Silene* sp.). The major shrubs found in

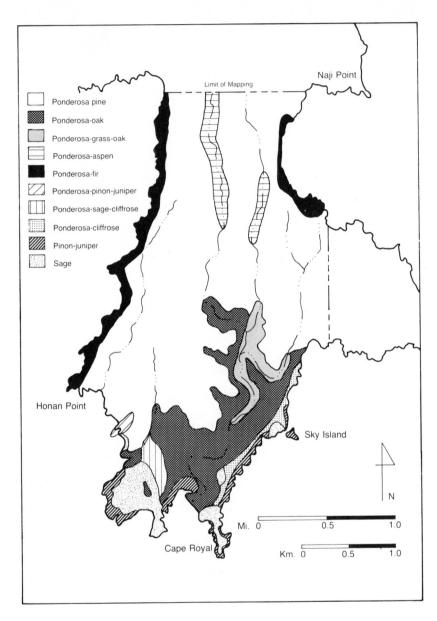

MAP 5. Vegetation of the Walhalla Glades.

FIG. 5. Sagebrush vegetation zone on Cape Royal.

the ponderosa pine forest are the previously mentioned Gambel oak, cliffrose *(Cowania mexicana),* which grows primarily along the southeastern edge of the Glades, and New Mexico locust *(Robinia neomexicana),* found in the northern portion of the study area.

In an area of relatively exclusive ponderosa forest in the vicinity of site GC408 (Map 3), a series of four transects averaging 360 m long were examined for vegetation cover (Stacy 1970). Along these transects, the ponderosa pine canopy cover averaged 41 percent, although the tree trunks themselves constituted ground cover of less than 1 percent. Gambel oak also made up less than 1 percent ground cover, and the remaining area was open grassland supporting Arizona fescue and lupine and other wildflowers. There also were two clumps of twelve to fifteen dead aspens and a group of eight living aspens.

The piñon-juniper association (Fig. 7), located only on the southern margins of the Walhalla Glades, normally has a range of 1,675–2,075 m (5,500–6,800 feet) with extensions to 2,200 m (7,250 feet) on exposed southern slopes (Rasmussen 1941:243). In reaching the edges of the Glades, this woodland exceeds even its usual extreme limit, perhaps because of the warm air rising from the canyon bottom. At this

FIG. 6. Two views of the ponderosa pine forest in the Walhalla Glades.

FIG. 7. Piñon-juniper vegetation zone on the southeastern edge of the Walhalla Glades.

elevation, however, the association is overwhelmingly dominated by piñon, which has a somewhat higher range than juniper, and immediately away from the rim of the canyon ponderosa pines begin to appear as well. Thus, the area designated on Map 5 as piñon-juniper woodland is probably better considered a transitional piñon-ponderosa forest. It is accompanied by a much denser ground cover than is the pure ponderosa pine forest, with a heavy understory of sagebrush, cliffrose, and Gambel oak. The last two species often grow to treelike heights near the edges of the Glades.

The piñon-juniper association characterizes the two rock pillars that were included in the study area—Sky Island and Wotan's Throne—and in those two locations the vegetation was examined in some detail (Stacy 1970). Sky Island, at about 2,377 meters, was dominated by piñon, which provided a canopy cover for 31 percent of the total surface area. Cliffrose covered another 15 percent of the area, curl-leaf mountain mahogany *(Cercocarpus ledifolius)* 13 percent, and serviceberry *(Amelanchier utahensis)* 8 percent. Only four juniper trees were found on Sky Island, and they appeared to be dying. On the steep northern exposure of the pillar grew four white firs and four Douglas firs, but no ponderosa pines were present. Other plant species noted but providing less than 1 percent ground cover were buffaloberry *(Shepherdia rotundifolia)*, gooseberry *(Ribes* sp.), Gambel oak, pricklypear cactus *(Optuntia* sp.), Indian ricegrass *(Oryzopsis hymenoides)*, and Mormon tea *(Ephedra* sp.).

On Wotan's Throne, at the slightly lower elevation of 2,316 meters, piñon was again predominant, forming canopy cover of 35–40 percent. However, junipers were more numerous here than in the higher areas, providing canopy cover for 2 percent of the surface area. The woodland was denser on Wotan's Throne than on Sky Island, with buffaloberry providing 15 percent ground cover, sagebrush about 10 percent, gooseberry and serviceberry about 15 percent, cliffrose, mountain mahogany, and Mormon tea together 10–15 percent, and cactus 5 percent. Clearly, to take full advantage of resources in the piñon-juniper association, the prehistoric inhabitants of the Walhalla Glades would have had to journey a short distance into the Grand Canyon to elevations where the woodland reaches its climax form.

Along the western margin of the Walhalla Glades, on sheltered north-facing slopes, and at elevations above 2,500 meters, white fir and Douglas fir begin to appear in the ponderosa forest. At about 2,530 meters, firs increase in number and within another 100 feet higher become the dominant species. To examine the pine-fir transition forest, a series of eleven transects, each measured at about 300 paces long, were walked along a ridgetop between a point 1.6 km south of site WP78 (Map 2) and a point 1.6 km north of the site (Stacy 1970). The elevational change between the two points was from about 2,500 to 2,548 meters.

At the southernmost observation station, ponderosa pine gave a canopy cover of about 58 percent, while 41 percent of the transect was unshaded grassland. Only a few scattered firs about 1 meter high were seen. This sort of vegetation prevailed as far north as WP78, except that aspen slowly became more common. From WP78 (2,530 m) north, firs began to increase at the expense of pine, although the grassland area remained extensive. However, 1.6 km north of the site, at 2,548 meters, the fir canopy cover suddenly increased to 42 percent and the forest became much denser, the open spaces decreasing to 19 percent of the transect. Pine cover was 24 percent, aspen 8 percent, and locust 5 percent. An additional transect examined at 2,560 meters showed that the trend toward fir dominance and heavier cover continued farther north.

As the ponderosa pine gives way to fir—though it never disappears completely— and the forest grows denser, temperatures drop, mosquitos and other insects become more numerous, and less sunlight filters through. All these factors would discourage both habitation and agricultural efforts and probably account for the apparent absence of these types of sites above 2,515 meters (8,250 feet).

Above 2,560 meters, blue spruce *(Picea pungens)* begins to appear and is in turn replaced by Engelmann spruce *(Picea engelmannii)* above 2,652 meters and eventually by alpine fir *(Abies lasiocarpa)*. However, aspen, white fir, Douglas fir, and even ponderosa pine continue to grow in locally favorable areas. This high forest of the Kaibab Plateau is occasionally interrupted by mountain meadows (Fig. 8) that occupy shallow valleys and are dominated by mountain muhly, sheep fescue *(Festuca ovina),* and other grasses and forbs (Merkle 1962:707).

WILD PLANT RESOURCES

In the ponderosa pine forest of the Walhalla Glades, 26 plant species producing edible leaves, fruits, nuts, or seeds were identified (Thornton 1969):

FIG. 8. Mountain meadow surrounded by spruce forest.

alumroot *(Huechera* sp.)
Arizona rose *(Rosa arizonica)*
blue flax *(Linum lewisii)*
bracken fern *(Pteridium aquilinum)*
bunchberry elder *(Sambucus microbotrys)*
columbine *(Aquilegia* sp.)
creeping mahonia *(Berberis repens)*
currant *(Ribes* sp.)
dandelion *(Taraxacum officinale)*
dock *(Rumex mexicanus)*
Gambel oak *(Quercus gambelii)*
goatsbeard *(Tragopogon dubius)*
lambsquarters *(Chenopodium album)*
lomatium *(Lomatium* sp.)
lupine *(Lupinus* sp.)
manzanita *(Arctostaphylos patula)*
mushrooms (several species)
onion *(Allium palmeri)*
prickly lettuce *(Lactuca serriola)*

28

raspberry *(Rubus* sp.*)*
scouring rush *(Equisetum arvense)*
sego-lilly *(Calochortus nuttallii)*
serviceberry *(Amelanchier polycarpa)*
strawberry *(Fragaria ovalis)*
tansy-mustard *(Descurainia* sp.*)*
wild celery *(Apium graveolens).*

No quantitative study of plant productivity was carried out, but casual observations suggested that none of the species listed occurs today in sufficient quantity to be an important food source. Within that limitation, the most abundant edible plants appeared to be dandelions, wild onions, lambsquarters, strawberries, raspberries, currants, manzanita, and acorns (Thornton 1969).

The only species in the near vicinity of the Walhalla Glades that was likely a major food source was the piñon with its crop of edible, protein-rich nuts. Gathering expeditions into the piñon-juniper woodland would also have found such high-yielding plants as datil yucca *(Yucca baccata),* Utah agave *(Agave utahensis),* and prickly-pear cactus *(Opuntia* sp.*).* In contrast, the higher fir and spruce forests produce few edible plants that cannot also be obtained in the ponderosa forest itself.

MODERN AND PREHISTORIC FAUNA

The fauna of the ponderosa pine forest consists of one major large mammal, the mule deer *(Odocoileus hemionus),* numerous species of small mammals such as mice, chipmunks, and squirrels, very few reptiles or amphibians, and a wide variety of birds. In the adjacent piñon-juniper association can be found other small mammals, including rabbits and hares, and on the rocky slopes of the Grand Canyon are bighorn sheep. The higher fir and spruce forests support many of the same species found in the ponderosa zone, though often in different frequencies, and only a few additional species of small mammals. Most of the following information about mammal species in the different plant communities has been taken from Rasmussen (1941).

Although the mule deer population at present is artificially high due to the removal of its natural predators by humans, this species was most likely an abundant food resource in prehistoric times. A migratory animal, the mule deer winters in the piñon-juniper zone from late September or October until April, when it begins to move into higher elevations. Only during the migration months of May and September–October is the herd concentrated in the ponderosa pine community, while the summer months find it spread throughout both the pine forest and the higher spruce-fir forest.

The primary carnivores of the ponderosa pine community are the coyote *(Canis latrans)* and the bobcat *(Lynx rufus)*, while the mountain lion *(Felis concolor)*, major predator of the deer herd, may be found along the rim of the Grand Canyon. The most abundant small mammals are Kaibab squirrels *(Sciurus kaibabensis)*, least and Beaver Mountain chipmunks *(Eutamias minimus* and *E. adsitus)*, golden-mantled ground squirrels *(Spermophilus lateralis)*, porcupines *(Erethizon dorsatum)*, and deer mice *(Peromyscus maniculatus)*. Relatively scarce species include the bushy-tailed wood rat *(Neotoma cinerea)*, the rock squirrel *(Sphermophilus variegatus)*, and Nuttall's cottontail *(Sylvilagus nuttallii)*.

On the slopes below the Walhalla Glades, in the piñon-juniper woodland, many of the same small mammals occur, and as mentioned earlier, mule deer are found in large herds during the winter. An important addition to the fauna is the black-tailed jackrabbit *(Lepus californicus)*, and the bushy-tailed wood rat is replaced by the desert wood rat *(Neotoma lepida)*. Even farther into the Grand Canyon, bighorn sheep *(Ovis canadensis)* inhabit the broken terrain and probably were more numerous in prehistoric times than they are today (Hoffmeister 1971:155–56).

The fauna found in the Walhalla Glades and the surrounding area today gives an indication of the range of species that would have been available to prehistoric hunters. Often, archaeological sites yield large amounts of animal bone from refuse deposits, showing which of the available species were actually used by the prehistoric inhabitants and perhaps suggesting the prevalence of different environmental conditions in the past. Unfortunately, this was not the case in the Walhalla Glades. The faunal sample was extremely small, with only five sites producing any animal bones. We originally assumed that the acid soil of the Glades had destroyed most of the bone, but because several human skeletons were found quite well preserved, we no longer feel certain that more animal bone ever existed. The faunal remains were extremely fragmented, with only a few pieces complete enough to allow any identification and even fewer identifiable at the species level (Table 2).

Taken at face value, the data in Table 2 suggest a heavy emphasis on the hunting of large mammals rather than small ones and considerable reliance on the canyon environment as represented by bighorn sheep, desert cottontail, and jackrabbit. However, if preservation was indeed poor, the small bones of mice, squirrels, rabbits, and hares would be more subject to destruction than would the larger bones of the artiodactyls, and thus the frequencies may be misleading. Because most of the

TABLE 2.
Faunal remains from the Walhalla Glades, in numbers of bones.

	GC212 &212A	GC215*	GC268	GC276	WP37
Bushy-tailed wood rat (*Neotoma* cf. *cinerea*)					1
Rock squirrel (cf. *Spermophilus variegatus*)				1	
Desert cottontail (*Sylvilagus auduboni*)	1				
Cottontail (*Sylvilagus* sp.)	2				
Jackrabbit (*Lepus* sp.; cf. *Lepus*)	4				
Mule deer (*Odocoileus hemionus*)	1				
Deer (*Odocoileus* sp.)		1			
Bighorn sheep (*Ovis canadensis*)	2	1			
Deer or bighorn sheep	5		1		
Artiodactyla	5	30		2	3
TOTAL	20	32	1	3	4

*A minimum of two individuals could account for all the bones in this sample (Richard W. Lang, personal communication).

artiodactyls could not be distinguished at the species level and because we do not know whether deer were hunted primarily on the plateau or in the piñon-juniper woodland of the canyon, the relative importance of deer and bighorn and of the plateau and canyon environments is uncertain. All that can safely be said is that both large and small mammals were hunted; that, not unexpectedly, the more important animal food sources seem to have been deer, bighorn, cottontails, and jackrabbits; and that hunters definitely exploited the fauna of the lower elevations. The remains of hunting camps around Greenland Lake demonstrate that hunting also took place in the higher fir and spruce forests.

EXPERIMENTAL GARDENS

In terms of agricultural potential, the Walhalla Glades today seem to be marginal at best. The growing season is short, the soils thin, rocky, and acid. Though total summer rainfall is probably just adequate for dryfarming, the dry season of April–June leaves little soil moisture available for seed germination. Yet the remains of numerous agricultural terraces on drainage valley slopes attest to some farming success by the prehistoric inhabitants.

To gain insight into the problems involved in cultivation on the plateau, experimental gardens were planted and maintained throughout both archaeological field seasons. In 1969, this effort was of a preliminary nature, designed simply to assess the feasibility of raising crops without irrigation of any sort. The following year's experiment was carried out more systematically to determine the effects of other variables in addition to moisture. Few quantitative measures of productivity could be obtained because the field season ended long before any plants had reached maturity, nor could certain variables such as soil fertility be controlled. The results of the experiment thus consist largely of qualitative observations about seed germination and early plant growth under varying conditions of sunlight, moisture, and cultivation technique.

In June, 1969, four plots were planted with modern varieties of corn, beans, and squash. Two of the gardens were located in the vicinity of site GC212, the other two at the terrace site WP19. On one occasion prior to the onset of the July rains, small amounts of water

32

(no more than 2 liters per hill of corn) were applied to portions of the gardens. Otherwise the plants were dependent solely upon the approximately 6 cm of rain that fell during the course of the experiment.

Under these conditions, none of the gardens was particularly successful. Germination was relatively low, and few of the plants that had sprouted were growing well at the end of the field season. Most were stunted and moderately to severely wilted. In some cases, poor soil or lack of sunlight might have contributed to these results, but the effect of such variables could not be assessed. The most successful garden was planted in the relatively deep alluvium of a drainage bed, where it probably received more moisture than any of the others.

The 1970 garden experiment again involved four plots, three of them situated on prehistoric terraces near site GC408 and the fourth in a low area between two ridges northwest of site GC276. The locations of the first three gardens were chosen with the aim of varying the direction of exposure and amount of sunlight received.

Garden 1, with a southern exposure, lay in a very open stand of ponderosa pine where it received full sunlight nearly all day. Its soil also seemed the richest in appearance and feel. With these characteristics, garden 1 was expected to be the most successful. Garden 2 stood in heavy shade in a dense pine forest, with a western exposure and dry, powdery, grayish brown soil. The third plot, in open ponderosa grassland, received sun during the morning and early afternoon because of its eastern exposure. Its soil was powdery, pale grayish brown, and rocky. Garden 4 was planted in a low, flat area of ponderosa grassland, where the presence of horsetail reeds (*Equisteum* sp.) indicated considerable soil moisture. A layer of cool air in this depression caused temperatures to remain about 5 degrees C below those elsewhere on the plateau.

The gardens were planted between June 19 and 23 in as nearly identical a manner as possible. Plots were divided into two separate 1.5 m by 3 m (5 ft. by 10 ft.) sections, and each was cleared of pine duff, weeds, and rocks. Before the seeds were planted, the soil was loosened to about 5 cm deep with a digging stick. Corn, bean, and squash seeds, a total of 743, had been obtained from the 1969 Hopi harvest; the exact sources and names of the varieties are not known.

Given the failure of the 1969 gardens, some artificial watering was deemed essential to the 1970 experiment. All gardens were watered two or three times a week until July 5, when the first heavy rain of the

33

summer fell. In each set of two plots, one plot received 28 liters (7.5 gal.) and the other 9.5 liters (2.5 gal.) at each watering, in order to permit comparison of the effects of differential irrigation.

The results of the 1970 experiment were much more positive than those of the preceding year, with higher germination rates and generally healthier plants. Of 400 corn seeds, 226 (56 percent) had sprouted by the final inspection on July 13, and it was felt that if these were early maturing varieties they would probably have yielded a harvest before the first frost. Squash and beans had lower germination success, 38 percent and 17 percent respectively.

Garden 2, the heavily shaded terrace garden, was unexpectedly the most successful, especially in its crop of beans. Its plot receiving 28 liters of water produced considerably more and larger plants than the one receiving 9.5 liters of water; in the former, 57 percent of all seeds sprouted, and average corn plant height was 12.6 cm (5 in.) at final check. In garden 3, the well-watered plot was relatively productive, while very few seeds sprouted in the section given less water. For the section given 28 liters of water, germination was 52 percent, corn seedling height an average 10.8 cm (4.25 in.). Garden 4, in the low, moist area, also did fairly well, with the plot receiving less water slightly more productive than its counterpart. Total germination in garden 4 was 53 percent, average corn plant height 9.3 cm (3.7 in.).

Surprisingly, the poorest results were obtained from garden 1, where no beans sprouted at all and the corn seemed rather unhealthy by mid-July. Little difference in germination was observed between the differentially watered plots, but corn in the section given 28 liters of water was much taller despite its poor appearance. Total germination for garden 1 was only 32 percent, and average corn height in the well-watered plot was 11.7 cm (4.6 in.).

These results support the previous year's conclusion that artificial watering, at least from the frost-free date of June 15 until the onset of the July rains, is essential to agriculture in the Walhalla Glades. In the plots given 9.5 liters of water, relatively little germination took place prior to the first rainfall, and seeds sprouting in mid-July were not likely to mature before the September frosts.

The poor performance of garden 1 with its full exposure to sunlight, in contrast to the success of shaded garden 2, demands some attempt at explanation. We had assumed at first that the ponderosa pine forest would be a hindrance to cultivation, and Hall (1942) had even proposed that the forest was absent in prehistoric times. However, the results from the experimental gardens suggest that the intensity of full, day-long sunlight at such high altitudes might actually be detrimental to plant growth and that the pines give the crops needed protection from the sun. Their shade may also prevent too-rapid evaporation of moisture from the soil. Alternatively, it is possible that poor soil fertility or some other uncontrolled variable accounted for the failure of garden 1.

The agricultural technique of terracing may have been an effective aid to cultivation in the Walhalla Glades. The experimental gardens planted in former terrace sites demonstrated that seeds germinate sooner and plants grow faster and healthier in the deeper soil at terrace edges than in the thinner soil upslope. It should also be noted that few problems were experienced with birds, rodents, or insect pests during the course of the experiment, although more damage might have occurred once the plants reached a larger size.

CULTIVATED PLANTS

That agriculture was practiced prehistorically with some degree of success is indicated not only by the artificial terraces scattered across the Walhalla Glades but also by the more direct evidence of charred corncobs and corn, bean, and squash pollen taken from excavated sites. Thirty corncobs or fragments of cobs were found in the fill of rooms at site GC212/212A. These included ten 8-rowed ears, nine 10-rowed, ten 12-rowed, and one 14-rowed specimen (Cutler and Blake 1980). Cupule width ranged from 7.5 mm to 8.6 mm, with a mean of 8.0 mm. The cobs were similar to others found in the Grand Canyon region, including specimens from Unkar Delta in the bottom of the canyon, suggesting that no special adaptation was required for the corn to grow at the relatively high elevation of the Walhalla Glades. A discussion of this corn and other plant materials from the Grand Canyon can be found in Cutler and Blake (1980).

Thirty-two pollen samples from thirteen sites in the Walhalla Glades were examined for cultigen pollen by Peter S. Bennett. Of these, at least thirteen samples from nine sites yielded pollen grains identified as corn *(Zea)*, bean *(Phaseolus)*, and squash *(Cucurbita)* (Table 3). The presence of all three types in samples from the fill behind terrace

TABLE 3.
Cultigen pollen in samples from the Walhalla Glades,
in number of grains.

Sample	Provenience	Corn (Zea)	Bean (Phaseolus)	Squash (Cucurbita)
GC212-11-8	Floor contact, room 11			1?
GC212A-62-3	Floor contact, room 62			1
GC215-4-3-10	Floor contact, room 4	3	1	
GC215-6-4-3	Floor contact, room 6	1		2
GC215-7-3-3	Floor contact, room 7	2	1	
GC215-10-4-4	Floor contact, room 10	2	5	
GC215-14-4-1	Wall mortar, room 14	1		
GC265-2-5	Floor contact, room 2	1		
GC268-3-15	Floor contact, room 3	2		
GC378-1-4	Floor contact, room 1			2
GC408-4	Fill of terrace	3		
GC408-10	Fill of terrace			1?
GC414A-2-5	Floor contact, room 2	2		
GC431-2	Fill of terrace		1	1
WP20-1-10	Base of fill in terrace		2	1

retaining walls indicates that all of these domesticated plants were
grown on the plateau prehistorically.

THE ECONOMIC POTENTIAL OF THE WALHALLA GLADES

If the prehistoric environment of the Walhalla Glades was similar to
that of today's—and we have no reason to think it was drastically different—then the Anasazi inhabitants must have found many of their needs
met in abundance. Raw materials for building and tool making were
certainly in no short supply, with friable limestone and sandstone
available for masonry construction and grinding tools; chert for chipped
stone tools; fallen timber and young trees for roofs and firewood; and
clay for mortar and pottery. Mule deer and various small mammals
could be hunted on the plateau, and a trip into the Grand Canyon

would net additional species, including bighorn sheep. The canyon would also have been a productive source of edible wild plants and, at least in some years, would have yielded a large harvest of piñon nuts.

In spite of this apparent abundance of resources, the Walhalla Glades are presently limited in two major ways. First, there is a decided lack of available surface water, with only one major spring located at the extreme southern tip of the plateau. Second, the spring drought that prevails today requires hand watering of newly planted gardens until the summer rains begin. It is hard for our twentieth-century minds to imagine anyone carrying water for this purpose over the four-mile round trip from, for example, site GC408 to Cliff Spring.

Present climatic conditions, however, do not necessarily reflect accurately those that prevailed nine hundred years ago. Tree-ring data from locations throughout the Southwest have been used by Dean and Robinson (1977) to show that precipitation in this region has been far from stable through time. Not only does annual precipitation vary greatly from year to year, but also the Southwest is subject to long periods of above-average or below-average moisture.

If the Walhalla Glades were inhabited at a time of higher precipitation than that of today's, the problems of water availability and spring drought might have been alleviated. More springs and seeps might have been active, and increased soil moisture from heavier winter snows might have sufficed for seed germination even if spring rainfall was still inadequate. Although any reconstruction of the prehistoric environment can only be speculative, there is some evidence that the Anasazi use of the Walhalla Glades may have coincided with periods of unusually high precipitation, and we will return to this evidence in our concluding chapter.

3
Settlement History

The history of settlement in the Walhalla Glades falls mainly between A.D. 1050 and 1150, with perhaps a few Pueblo farmers in the area as much as a hundred years earlier. These dates are based on pottery recovered during the SAR survey and excavations and on the survey collections of Edward T. Hall. Although nine tree-ring specimens were dated by the Laboratory of Tree-Ring Research of the University of Arizona, only one gave an actual cutting date, and all the dates were considerably earlier or later than those indicated by ceramics found at the sites. Stone implements found near Greenland Lake to the north of the Glades suggested that Basketmaker people also used the region sporadically between about 100 B.C. and A.D. 500, and these artifacts will be discussed in Chapter 5. Here we are concerned with the Pueblo occupation of the Glades as it is represented by the architectural remains of habitation, storage, and farming activities (Table 4).

Evidence of Pueblo use of the Walhalla Glades before about A.D. 1050 is scarce, consisting only of a few potsherds of types dating prior to that time. These sherds usually were found in association with later ceramics at sites that probably dated after A.D. 1050. Only one site recorded by Hall in 1939 had an entire collection that seemed consistent with a date of A.D. 950–1050, according to Marshall's reexamination of the sample of 53 sherds, and only one site excavated by SAR appeared to date slightly before A.D. 1050. Thus we have some indication that a few people were using the Glades before that time, but we can say little about the distribution or characteristics of the sites or about the nature of the economic adaptation.

The major occupation of the area began around A.D. 1050 and lasted until about A.D. 1100. During this period, sites reached their greatest number, including at least 64 that could be dated, and their maximum density over the plateau. Both habitation sites and their associated agricultural terraces tended to lie along the ridgetops bordering drainage valleys, perhaps because these gentle slopes allowed a combination of water retention and erosion control that would have been difficult to maintain on the steep slopes of the valleys. Dwellings were usually small structures of one or two rectangular masonry rooms with few interior or outlying features such as hearths or storage cists. Certain characteristics of the habitation sites suggest that they were used for fairly short periods of time, probably only in the summer. There seem to have been no kivas present.

Around A.D. 1100, the number of sites apparently declined considerably, only 20 of them being datable ceramically to the interval between A.D. 1100 and 1150. Sites did tend to become slightly larger, with two or three rooms the norm, and two excavated sites were much larger; but the total number of rooms still decreased, presumably reflecting a drop in population. Site configuration and methods of construction changed little from the preceding period. Despite a trend toward abandonment of the western margin of the Walhalla Glades, site locations also remained generally the same as in the preceding period; that is, on the edges of ridges above the drainage valleys that cross the Glades from north to south. However, expansion took place onto several rock pillars standing away from the rim of the plateau, indicating some change in adaptation within a continuing agricultural framework. Like the rest of the Grand Canyon region, the Walhalla Glades were abandoned by the inhabitants around A.D. 1150 or slightly earlier.

The remainder of this chapter will describe each of the periods of Pueblo use of the Walhalla Glades, focusing on (1) the dating of each time period, (2) the distribution of sites across the Glades, (3) site configuration, or the kinds and combinations of architectural features found at the sites, and (4) methods of architectural construction. Agricultural terraces will be discussed separately because few of them could be dated to a specific time period.

TABLE 4.
Sites recorded during the SAR survey and excavations.

Site	Type of Site	Date (A.D.)	Tested or Excavated	Survey Only
GC212, 212A	Group of 6 rooms + group of 3 rooms	1100–1150	X	
GC215 (WP1)	18 rooms in 4 groups	1100–1150	X	
GC264 (WP51)	2 rooms + alignment	post–1050		X
GC265 (WP52)	4 rooms	1100–1150	X	
GC268 (WP54)	At least 2 rooms + terraces	1050–1100	X	
GC269 (WP55)	Probably 2 rooms	post–1050		X
(WP56)	At least 1 room	post–1050		X
GC270	1 room	950–1050?	X	
GC276	Rock shelter		X	
GC309	At least 3 rooms	1050–1100	X	
GC326	Uncertain		X	
GC329B	2 rooms	1050–1100	X	
GC378	1 room	1050–1100	X	
GC408	2 rooms	1050–1100	X	
GC414A	1 room	1050–1100	X	
WP2	3 large bifaces			X
WP3	1 large biface			X
WP4	1 large biface			X
WP5	Lithic concentration		X	
WP6	Lithic scatter			X
WP7–WP11	Pictographs			X
WP12	1 room or terrace			X
WP13	Possible terrace			X
WP14	1 room	post–1050	X	
WP15	4 rooms		X	
WP16	Probably 1 room			X
WP17	1 room + terraces			X
WP18	1 room		X	
WP19	Terraces			X
WP20	Terraces		X	

41

TABLE 4 *(continued).*

Site	Type of Site	Date (A.D.)	Tested or Excavated	Survey Only
WP21	Probably 1 room			X
WP22	Sherd and lithic scatter		X	
WP23	Probably 1 room			X
WP24	2–3 roomblocks	post–1050		X
WP25	1 alignment			X
WP26	Possible terraces			X
WP27	Check dams			X
WP28	2 rooms			X
WP29	1 biface fragment			X
WP30	1 room			X
WP31	At least 1 room			X
WP32	Terraces			X
WP33	Rubble mound			X
WP34	Rectangular stone outline	post–1050		X
WP35	1 room			X
WP36	Stone-ringed circular depression		X	
WP37	3 rooms in overhang	post–1050	X	
WP38	Rubble mound			X
WP39	Rubble mound			X
WP40	Rubble mound			X
WP41	2 rooms			X
WP43	Rubble mound			X
WP44	2 rooms			X
WP45	Crescent-shaped pile of cobbles			X
WP46	At least 5 rooms	post–1050		X
WP47	Probably 3 rooms			X
WP48	Pile of large stones			X
WP49	1 room			X
WP50	3 rooms			X
WP53	Terraces		X	

TABLE 4 *(continued)*.

Site	Type of Site	Date (A.D.)	Tested or Excavated	Survey Only
WP57	Terraces			X
WP58	Possible room			X
WP59	Terraces			X
WP60	Rubble mound			X
WP61	Rubble mound			X
WP62	Boulder alignment	post–1050		X
WP63	Rubble mound			X
WP64	Rubble mound			X
WP65	Scatter of rubble			X
WP66	Rubble mound			X
WP67	2 rooms		X	
WP68	Check dam			X
WP69	Rubble mound			X
WP70	3 lithic artifacts			X
WP72	1 room	post–1050	X	
WP78	Sherd scatter	post–1050		X
WP79	Probably 1 room			X
WP80	Rubble mound			X
WP81	Rubble mound			X
WP82	Rubble mound			X
KP1	1 room		X	
WT1	Lithic scatter			X
WT2	1 room		X	
WT3	Granary			X
WT4	Possible granary			X
WT5	1 room			X
WT6	Semicircular alignment			X
WT7	Stone wall			X
WT8	Sherds from 1 pot			X
WT9	Possible terrace			X
WT10	1 room			X

A.D. 950–1050

In his survey report, Hall (1942:19) noted that 18 percent of his 6,480 "Arizona" (Kayenta Branch) potsherds "were representative of Pueblo I and earlier." These sherds included a few specimens identified as Lino Gray, which was extant between A.D. 575 and 875 (Breternitz 1966), and Kana'a Gray and Kana'a Black-on-white (A.D. 760–900 and A.D. 725–950, respectively; Breternitz 1966). In classifying the ceramics recovered during the SAR survey and excavations and in reexamining Hall's collections, Marshall recognized no Lino Gray sherds. Still, on the basis of surface collections, he was able to assign ten of Hall's sites to the Pueblo I period, or between A.D. 875 and 950. The diagnostic types were Kana'a Gray, Kana'a Black-on-white, Floyd Gray, Deadmans Black-on-red, Coconino Gray, and Medicine Gray, although the last three extend well into the Pueblo II period, with end dates of about A.D. 1060 (Breternitz 1966). At the outset of the project, then, ten sites were considered good possibilities for representing a pre-A.D. 1050 occupation of the Walhalla Glades.

Two of these sites, GC270 and GC378, were excavated, and another, GC326, was tested. Only GC270, a one-room structure, yielded a ceramic sample that was entirely consistent with a pre-A.D. 1050 date, whereas the other two sites produced some sherds of definite later date (see Tables 7 and 8, Chapter 4). Even at GC270, the "early" sherds were few, and the bulk of the pottery, including the types Tusayan Corrugated, Deadmans Gray, Walhalla Corrugated, and Shinarump Brown, was either nondiagnostic or suggestive of dates well after A.D. 950. In addition, small amounts of early pottery types appeared at other sites that clearly dated between A.D. 1050 and 1100 or even between A.D. 1100 and 1150. Thus, with respect to Pueblo I sites, the excavation and testing program tended not to bear out the preliminary dating from the surface collections. Of the unexcavated sites given preliminary early dates, only one (GC339), a two-room structure located on the southwestern edge of the Glades, had a relatively large ceramic sample that could have fallen between A.D. 950 and 1050. The others produced surface collections too small to permit any reliable dating.

Given these considerations, we can say only that it seems likely that a few Pueblo people were using the Walhalla Glades sometime between A.D. 950 and 1050. The meager data for this period do not permit a discussion of site distribution, and any details about site configuration and construction technique are provided by a single site, GC270 (Fig. 9). This room, located on the edge of a broad ridgetop near the center of the Glades, had a floor area of approximately 10.2 square meters. Its remaining limestone masonry walls stood no more than two courses high but were built in an interesting variety of styles: two walls of limestone blocks laid horizontally, another of vertically placed blocks, and the fourth of limestone cobbles overlaid by horizontally placed slabs and blocks. Fallen wall rubble was insufficient to have brought the walls to more than 1 meter in height, but no evidence for an adobe or wood-and-brush (jacal) superstructure was seen. A circular, unplastered fire pit was found in the clay floor of the room. The fact that the sides of the pit were not heavily fired suggested that this hearth was not used to heat the room through the severe winters of the plateau. Furthermore, the shallowness of the fill, the scarcity of trash in the room, and the apparent absence of any outside activity areas indicated that the use of the room was short-lived.

In all respects, site GC270 was similar to the excavated sites that

FIG. 9. Site GC270, view to the northwest.

dated after A.D. 1050, and it may represent the early end of the known habitation sequence of the Walhalla Glades. If so, the site exemplifies the beginning of a trend toward small structures probably inhabited only during the summer months by Anasazi who were farming on the plateau.

A.D. 1050–1100

One of the primary ceramic markers for the period from A.D. 1050 to 1100 is Tsegi Orange Ware. Most sherds of this ware were unidentifiable at the type level, so we have used the date A.D. 1050, when the earliest type, Tusayan Black-on-red, first began to be manufactured (Breternitz 1966:99), as the beginning date for this time period. Two other diagnostic types are Sosi Black-on-white and Dogoszhi Black-on-white of Tusayan White Ware. Breternitz (1966:73,96) gives beginning dates of A.D. 1075 and 1085, respectively, for these types but notes that Sosi Black-on-white is poorly dated. Colton (1955) places the appearance of both types at A.D. 1070. The criterion for the end date of the period from 1050 to 1100 is the absence of Flagstaff Black-on-white, which was being produced by at least A.D. 1100 (Breternitz 1966:75). Finally, the predominance of Black Mesa Black-on-white in the Tusayan White Ware category and of Tusayan Corrugated among the unpainted pottery types (Table 7, Chapter 4) is also consistent with the date of A.D. 1050–1100 (Fig. 10).

Among the 25 sites excavated or tested by SAR, six could be dated with some confidence to this time period. In addition, Marshall assigned to this interval 58 of the sites recorded by Hall, for a total of 64 sites. We should note, however, that the total figure should be viewed with reservations and regarded as an expression of the order of magnitude of settlement size. This qualification stems from the proximity of many one-room or two-room structures in the Walhalla Glades, which often made it difficult to decide where to draw boundaries between sites. Hall, in his 1939 survey, apparently attempted to deal with this problem by assigning to nearby features a single number but suffixing one of the features with an "A" and in some cases a "B": for example, GC329, GC329A, and GC329B. Our policy, on the other hand, was generally to assign separate numbers to all features that were not obviously associated with one another.

In counting sites for the purposes of this report, we have used the

46

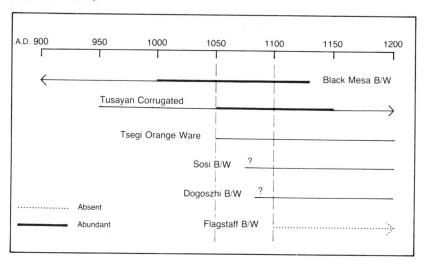

FIG. 10. Pottery types used in dating sites between A.D. 1050 and 1100. Dates are based on those given by Breternitz (1966).

following procedure. If two or more noncontiguous rooms were included by Hall under one site number not divided by suffixes, we assumed that they were closely associated enough to warrant counting them as one site. If, instead, he assigned an "A" or "B" suffix to one or more rooms, we counted those features as a separate site. Consequently, our total of 64 sites dated between A.D. 1050 and 1100 may, depending on one's bias, seem either too low, since it includes 11 sites each of several noncontiguous rooms, or too high, since it includes 17 sites with "A" or "B" suffixes that might otherwise have been lumped together as 8 sites. Nevertheless, the total number of dated structures—at least 116 rooms—is such that no matter how they are counted, they obviously attest to a high site density during the half-century from A.D. 1050 to 1100.

Site Distribution

Map 6 shows the locations of the sites dated between A.D. 1050 and 1100. The site distribution suggests that there was a preference among the prehistoric inhabitants not for any particular geographic portion of the Walhalla Glades but for a specific kind of topographic situation. That is, sites almost always occur near the edges of the broad ridges that separate the drainage valleys or toward the centers of the narrower

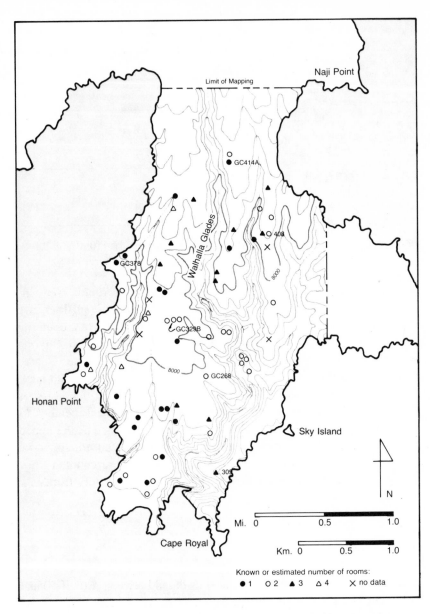

MAP 6. Locations of sites dated between A.D. 1050 and 1100.

ridges. None of the dated sites and few of the undated ones (see Map 4, Chapter 1) lie on the steep valley slopes or in the drainage beds.

The distribution of habitation sites in the Glades is probably a function of the agricultural focus of the prehistoric economy. As Map 7 shows, the locations of known agricultural terraces and check dams generally coincide with those of the habitation sites. The terraces shown on the map are only a few of the total in the Walhalla Glades because neither the SAR survey nor that by Hall emphasized the numbering of these features as sites. Although none of the terraces by themselves could be dated ceramically, at least twelve of them lay adjacent to or very near apparent habitation sites that could be dated between A.D. 1050 and 1100.

The ridgetop locations offer gently sloping terrain where some precipitation runoff could be caught by the terraces and check dams but where the danger of erosion would be much less than on the steep valley slopes. Because of the shallowness of the soil of the plateau, erosion was probably a major concern to the prehistoric farmers, and the terraces may have been as important for erosion control as for water conservation. The locations of the terraces also suggest that the Walhalla Glades were used during periods of above-average precipitation between A.D. 1050 and 1100. Without greater precipitation than that of the mid-1900s, it seems unlikely that the ridgetops would have received sufficient runoff to support crops or that the heads of the minor drainages, where the only recorded check dams are located (Map 7), would have provided adequate water for floodwater farming.

It appears, then, that agricultural features were situated wherever local topography provided advantageous conditions for water and erosion control and that habitation and/or storage sites were located near the agricultural fields. Given the proximity of habitations to terraces, we might infer that farmland was in adequate supply and that despite the high site density, population pressure was not great enough to require that dwellings be built away from the fields in areas unsuitable for cultivation.

Site Configuration

A list of all the kinds of sites found in the Walhalla Glades would include diverse features ranging from pictographs to inhabited rock-shelters and from cliff granaries to sherd and lithic concentrations.

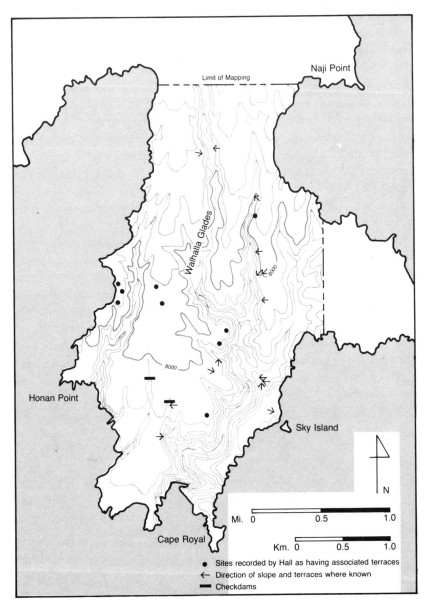

MAP 7. Locations of recorded agricultural terraces and check dams.

However, the overwhelming majority of the sites, especially those that could be dated between A.D. 1050 and 1100, were what we refer to as habitation sites—that is, the architectural remains of one or more rooms that we assume were used either as dwellings or as storage facilities or both. Next most numerous, even though many of them were not assigned individual site numbers, were the agricultural terraces and check dams. The agricultural sites will be described in a later section; here we are concerned with the sites presumed to be habitations.

Among the sites for which we have data about site configuration, either from our own records or from Hall's, 75 percent of those dating between A.D. 1050 and 1100 consisted of only one or two rooms (Table 5). Three-room sites accounted for 18 percent of the total, and four-room sites, 7 percent. None of the dated sites were known to have more than four rooms.

Whenever two or more rooms were present, they were usually built contiguous to one another, either in a straight row or in an L-shaped arrangement; this was the case in 75 percent of this type of site. These adjacent structures tended to include one or occasionally two large rooms and one or more small ones. For the sites known only from survey, of course, we have no precise room measurements, and "large" and "small" are relative evaluations. However, we do have measurements for seven rooms at six sites of this time period that were

TABLE 5.
Numbers of sites of different sizes.

	1 Room	2 Rooms	3 Rooms	4 Rooms	More than 4 Rooms	No Data
A.D. 1050–1100						
Sites recorded by Hall	21	19	10	4	–	4
Sites excavated by SAR	2	3	1	–	–	–
TOTAL	23	22	11	4	–	4
A.D. 1100–1150						
Sites recorded by Hall	1	7	7	–	–	2
Sites excavated by SAR	–	–	–	1	2	–
TOTAL	1	7	7	1	2	2

completely or partially excavated: GC268, GC309, GC329B, GC378, GC408, and GC414A.*

The sizes of the excavated rooms ranged from 3.7 m² to 10.8 m² of floor space, with a mean of 7.0 m². At the two one-room sites, GC378 (Fig. 11) and GC414A, room size was close to the mean: 7.8 m² and 6.8 m², respectively. Site GC408 consisted of two rooms (Fig. 12), the larger measuring 10.8 m² and the smaller, 5.4 m². At site GC329B (Fig. 13), the larger of two rooms had an area of 9.3 m², while the smaller room was unexcavated. Site GC309 (Fig. 14) was a three-room structure of one large and two small rooms, with one of the latter measuring 3.7 m². Finally, the only excavated room at GC268 (Fig. 15), one of at least two rooms present, had a floor area of 5.5 m².

Only the largest room excavated, room 2 at site GC408, contained a hearth, and other interior features were also extremely scarce in the excavated rooms of this time period. They consisted entirely of four shallow depressions in the floors of two rooms. Three of these occurred in the excavated room at site GC268, the largest of them measuring 93 cm in diameter and none of them more than 9 cm deep. The fourth, found in the single room at GC414A, was equally large and 15 cm deep. These features were obviously too shallow to have served as true storage cists, but their actual function or origin is unknown.

At sites GC378 and GC408, extensive areas of overburden were removed outside the rooms in an effort to discover any exterior features or activity zones that might have been present. Only one such outlying feature was found, a low, L-shaped wall extending out from the smaller room at GC408. This wall did not seem to be part of a complete room or other roofed structure, and although it might have served to shelter an outside work area, no associated features were found in the tested areas near the wall. At site GC309, a large, circular depression outside the roomblock was tested to determine whether it might represent a kiva or other structure. A layer of culturally sterile clay overlying bedrock was encountered at a depth of only 12 cm, effectively ending this line of conjecture.

In general, the excavations indicated that habitation sites of the period from A.D. 1050 to 1100 were rather barren structures, little more than empty rooms with few features that might have been used in

---

*Plan drawings of these and other excavated sites accompany the site descriptions in Appendix A.

FIG. 11. Site GC378, view to the northwest.

FIG. 12. Site GC408, view to the southeast.

FIG. 13. Excavated room at site GC329B, view to the south.

FIG. 14. Excavated room at site GC309, view to the northeast.

domestic activities. Three rooms that had apparently burned contained ground stone implements and broken pots in their fallen roof debris, as if these objects had been lying on the roofs when they collapsed. These artifacts provide some evidence for food processing at sites GC329B and GC414A, and especially at GC408, where artifacts were most numerous in the larger room. Still, the functions of the rooms themselves are less than clear.

The large room containing a hearth at GC408 can probably be classified with some justification as a domiciliary structure, assuming that heated rooms or ones where cooking took place were rooms that were actually lived in. Small rooms without fire pits, on the other hand, might legitimately be labeled storage structures. These functional interpretations fit well with the usual combination of one large room and one or two small rooms at the multiroom sites. It is with the large or average-sized rooms lacking hearths, particularly those rooms that were the only ones at sites, that we have difficulty interpreting function. As already mentioned, the artifact assemblages from the large room at GC329B and from GC414A suggested the possibility of some activities other than storage. Yet cultural material was not abundant

FIG. 15. Site GC268. Top: excavated room, view to the north; note agricultural terraces at upper right. Bottom: test trench across agricultural terraces.

even at these sites and was scarcer still at all other sites but GC408. Combined with the paucity of features inside or outside the rooms, this evidence suggests that any domestic functions of the rooms were occasional and that people did not live at these sites for long periods of time.

On balance, our interpretation of the sites dating between A.D. 1050 and 1100 is that they functioned as summer farmsteads used for temporary shelter and for storage of crops by people whose winter homes were elsewhere. The scarcity of hearths in the rooms prompts our interpretation of seasonality, given the severe winter weather of the plateau. The farmers probably built well-sealed masonry rooms for the protection of their harvested crops and used these rooms or additional ones for shelter when needed. Some processing of the plants probably also took place, but on the whole we would hypothesize that domestic activities were fairly minimal.

Another reasonable conjecture is that one habitation site such as GC408 might have been used by an individual or family who had fields scattered in a number of places, with other, one-room storage structures near those fields. That is, there is no particular reason to believe that every site in the Walhalla Glades belonged to a separate individual or family or, furthermore, that all the sites were in use at the same time. However, this conjecture is purely speculative, and it still seems likely that the interval between A.D. 1050 and 1100 was when the Glades were most intensively farmed by the greatest number of people.

Construction Methods

The six excavated sites provided information about construction methods as well as site configuration for the time period between A.D. 1050 and 1100. The generalizations drawn from these sites also apply to most of the undated sites that were excavated or tested, since building techniques tended to be quite uniform across the Walhalla Glades and through time.

All of the rooms dating to this period, and indeed all of the architectural features found in the Walhalla Glades, were built from the abundant limestone of the Kaibab formation. Several quarry sites were seen in places where the limestone outcropped at the ground surface, and one site, WP48, appeared to be a pile of stones that had been trans-

57

ported to a building site but never used. A typical room had walls of limestone slabs and blocks, many of which had been shaped by chipping or pecking, laid horizontally in adobe mortar on the original ground surface. Within this general pattern, the walls varied in their regularity of coursing, evenness of alignment on their inside or outside faces, and other details. A few foundation courses consisted of upright rather than horizontally placed slabs, and the foundations of the excavated room at GC268 were laid in shallow trenches. However, the overall uniformity of construction can probably be attributed to the homogeneity of the building material; that is, there are only so many ways in which a piece of limestone can be used to build a wall.

At two of the sites, GC309 and GC378, there was sufficient fallen wall rubble around the excavated rooms to have raised the walls to about 1.5 meters high, or probably fully to the roof. In the big room at GC408 were large amounts of burned, beam-impressed adobe that were identified during excavation as representing jacal walls above the masonry foundations. The charred remains of two probable corner posts indicated that additional support had been required for the roof of this room.

Two postholes containing charred posts were also found in the excavated room at GC329B, but there was no evidence in this room, the small room at GC408, or at sites GC268 and GC414A either for jacal superstructures or for sufficient wall fall to have formed walls more than 1 meter high. Since the excavated rooms at GC329B and GC414A had apparently burned and contained obvious roof fall, it is probably safe to assume that they did not also have upper walls of combustible wood or brush that would have left charred remains. It is possible that these rooms once had walls entirely of stone that had been dismantled and reused in construction by later residents of nearby sites, but we really have no explanation beyond conjecture for the absence of complete wall remains at many of the sites.

No evidence of entryways into any of the excavated rooms was found, either in the direct form of doorways or in the indirect form of cover slabs for doorways or roof hatchways. Floors usually consisted simply of the naturally occurring layer of clay on which the rooms were built. At site GC268, this surface was covered with a thin layer of prepared adobe, and in the excavated room at GC329B, with sandy soil. As mentioned earlier, floor features included only one hearth, which was a circular, basin-shaped pit lined with cobbles at its base.

Finally, charred beam fragments on the floor at GC329B and charcoal and burned adobe, some of it with beam impressions, in the rooms at GC408 and GC414A indicated that roofs were constructed of beams overlaid by smaller poles and covered with earth.

A.D. 1100–1150

Sites dating after A.D. 1100 in the Walhalla Glades were distinguished from earlier sites by one key pottery type, Flagstaff Black-on-white of Tusayan White Ware. According to Breternitz (1966:75), the Flagstaff design style was established by A.D. 1100 at the latest, so we assigned that date to the beginning of the final phase of occupation on the plateau (Fig. 16). Other ceramics diagnostic of this period were Sosi Black-on-white and Dogoszhi Black-on-white, when found in association with Flagstaff Black-on-white. After A.D. 1100, Sosi and Dogoszhi were far more abundant than the earlier Black Mesa Black-on-

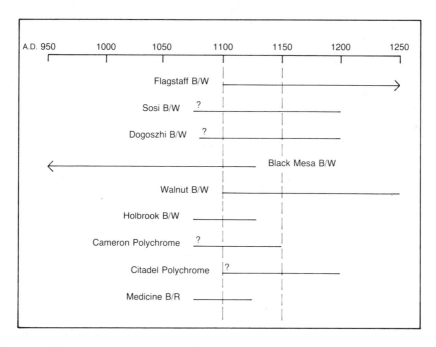

FIG. 16. Pottery types used in dating sites between A.D. 1100 and 1150. Dates are based on those given by Breternitz (1966).

white. With its end date of about A.D. 1130 (Breternitz 1966:70), Black Mesa Black-on-white also helped fix the terminal date for this period at roughly A.D. 1150, assuming that the type did not reach extinction until some years after its manufacture had ceased. Along the same lines of reasoning, traces of the Little Colorado White Ware types Walnut Black-on-white, which appeared about A.D. 1100 (Colton 1955), and Holbrook Black-on-white, which ended about A.D. 1130 (Breternitz 1966:78), lent support to the range of dates assigned to this period of settlement. Similar evidence was also provided by several of the types of Tsegi Orange Ware. The final date of the period is less definite than the initial one, but we feel certain that the plateau was abandoned by at least A.D. 1150, if not somewhat earlier.

A total of twenty sites could be dated ceramically between A.D. 1100 and 1150, including three that were extensively excavated by SAR (GC212/212A, GC215, and GC265) and seventeen dated by Marshall on the basis of Hall's survey collections. The sites were counted according to the same procedure used for those of the preceding period, except that the two excavated roomblocks numbered GC212 and GC212A, situated only 11 meters apart, were considered a single site. All together the sites comprised at least 67 rooms, considerably fewer than found for the preceding period.

Although the few small structures found on Wotan's Throne, the isolated rock pillar included in the site survey, were not counted among the dated sites, it seemed likely that use of the Throne was generally after A.D. 1100. Few potsherds were found there, but they included one Moenkopi Corrugated vessel and 15 other sherds of that type, which was virtually absent from the Walhalla Glades until A.D. 1100. All other sherds were of Shinarump Gray Ware, which appeared in small amounts prior to A.D. 1100 but did not become abundant until after that time. The evidence, then, is scant, but it is entirely consistent with a date of post-A.D. 1100 for the expansion onto Wotan's Throne.

Site Distribution

For the settlement between A.D. 1100 and 1150 we have fewer sites with which to determine preferred locations, but again it appears that structures were located in virtually all areas of the Walhalla Glades (Map 8). However, it also seems that some abandonment of the west-

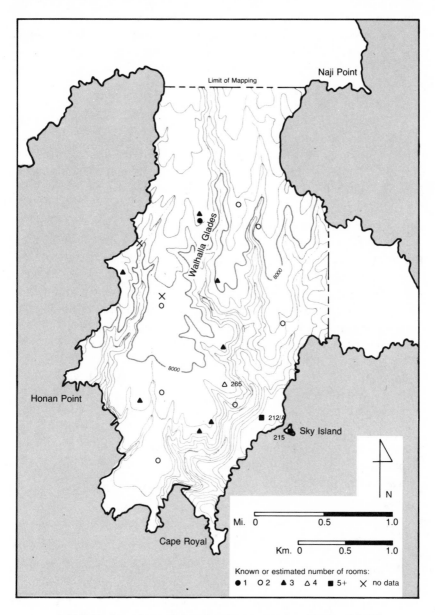

MAP 8. Locations of sites dated between A.D. 1100 and 1150.

ern and northern sectors took place in favor of land to the southeast, where most of the terrain consists of the relatively wide, deep valley of the lower Walhalla Glades drainage. The number of dated sites there was 58 percent of the number known from that sector between A.D. 1050 and 1100, whereas the post-A.D. 1100 sites in the west and northeast comprised only 24 percent and 28 percent, respectively, of the number of sites dated to the preceding period.

The topographic placement of the dated sites remained much as it had been during the earlier period of settlement, that is, on the fairly gently sloping or even flat ridgetops overlooking the drainages. From this observation, we might assume that the agricultural adaptation also remained unchanged. Yet another possibility arises because according to Hall's survey data, the southeastern quadrant of the Glades is the only area where sites tended to occur on the lower slopes or even in the bottoms of the drainages (see Map 4, Chapter 1). None of these sites could be dated ceramically, but given the hypothesized shift of site distribution in this direction after A.D. 1100, many of the valley sites possibly belonged to that period. If so, they represent a significant change in the choice of topography for site location and presumably an attempt to harness greater amounts of runoff than could be caught on the ridgetops. Still, we have no reliable way to date these sites, and on the basis of dated sites alone, we cannot postulate any shift in topographic situation.

A more definite indication of change in adaptation between A.D. 1100 and 1150 was the expansion of settlement onto the rock pillars, Sky Island and Wotan's Throne. We are not certain what advantages these locations offered, but their use might have been associated with exploitation of the piñon-juniper woodland or with their slightly lower elevation than that of the plateau.

Site Configuration

Between A.D. 1100 and 1150, sites continued to be mainly habitation or storage rooms and agricultural terraces. The one-room sites that were previously so common were seldom built after A.D. 1100, and only three of the dated sites had two or more noncontiguous rooms. The usual number was two or three rooms, and together these kinds of sites made up 78 percent of those for which we have size information

(Table 5). Not only did average size increase somewhat but also several sites were much larger than usual. Site GC212/212A (Figs. 17 and 18) consisted of two roomblocks, one containing four main rooms (GC212) and the other, three (GC212A). Next to the four main rooms of GC212 had later been constructed two small rooms, for a total of nine at the entire site. GC215 was even larger, with eighteen rooms divided into four roomblocks (Figs. 19, 20, and 21). We cannot be certain that no equally large but undatable sites existed during the preceding period. Nevertheless, it appears from the available data that these large sites departed considerably from the average site size of either period of settlement.

As in the preceding period, sites composed of more than a single room tended to combine one or more large rooms with one or more small ones. This pattern was true for most of the sites known from Hall's survey and for two excavated sites, GC212/212A and GC265 (Fig. 22). At the Sky Island site, GC215, all rooms were relatively small but still occurred in varying sizes within the roomblocks.

For determining average room size during the period from A.D. 1100

FIG. 17. Site GC212, Walhalla Ruin, view to the northwest.

63

FIG. 18. Site GC212A during excavation, view to the southeast.

FIG. 19. Site GC215, roomblock A, view to the west.

64

FIG. 20. Site GC215, roomblock B, view to the northeast.

FIG. 21. Site GC215, roomblock C, view to the north.

FIG. 22. Site GC265, view to the southeast.

to 1150, we may not have a particularly representative sample of excavated sites. GC212/212A and GC215, as already mentioned, were quite different from the other known sites in their total numbers of rooms. Only site GC265, consisting of three contiguous rooms in a linear block and a noncontiguous fourth room, approximated the standard size of this period. Judging from this site alone, rooms appear to have increased in size after A.D. 1100, with a range from 7.9 m² to 13.3 m² of floor space and a mean of 10.5 m².

If all three excavated sites are considered—a total of 27 measured rooms—average room size drops to 7.7 m², not much more than the mean 7.0 m² of the preceding period. On the other hand, the range of room sizes at all sites was much greater than for the earlier period, the smallest measuring 1.1 m² and the largest 24.2 m². The full spectrum of sizes was found at site GC212/212A, where the rooms ranged from 1.4 m² to 24.2 m² in area, with a mean of 11 m². This average, like that for site GC265, indicated a trend toward larger rooms after A.D. 1100. Site GC215 fell at the lower end of the size range, with rooms from 1.1 m² to 8.8 m² in floor space and an average size of only 4.8 m². With its unusual location and size, GC215 was the least comparable of the excavated sites to the rest of the dated sample and probably does not negate the other evidence for construction of larger rooms after A.D. 1100.

Though room size apparently changed somewhat after A.D. 1100, rooms did not change much in terms of interior or exterior features, which continued to be scarce. Only one of the 15 excavated rooms at GC215 contained a fire pit, and it was not one of the larger rooms but fell closer to average at 5.5 m². All other rooms at this site were completely devoid of interior features. Despite extensive surface stripping outside the roomblocks, the only exterior feature found at GC215 was an L-shaped wall adjoining the largest roomblock. At GC265, no interior features were found, even in the largest of the three excavated rooms, nor were there any outlying features in the extensive area cleared outside the rooms. Three large, circular depressions outside the roomblock at GC265 were tested on the chance that they represented kivas, but like the similar depression at site GC309, these extended only some 20 cm to bedrock. Presumably these depressions and many like them at other sites were borrow pits from which the prehistoric builders had quarried clay.

Site GC212/212A showed something of an exception to the general scarcity of features. Each of the four large rooms at GC212 contained one or two hearths, and outside roomblock GC212A was a large fire pit that had probably served as a roasting oven. It was associated with a use surface and an outlying wall that had apparently supported a ramada or partial shelter adjoining the roomblock. Also found at this site were seventeen depressions, seven of them in rooms, six in the area between roomblocks GC212 and GC212A, and the remaining four partially beneath the walls of roomblock GC212. None of the depressions was more than 28 cm deep, too shallow to have served as storage cists, and that four of them clearly predated the construction of GC212 again suggested that these features were borrow pits. The location of the depressions in rooms probably resulted simply from the rooms' having been built over the earlier pits, although we cannot entirely rule out the possibility that the depressions served some as yet undiscovered function inside rooms.

Another group of unusual features at site GC212 was a series of 25 roughly rectangular enclosures formed of fallen wall rubble on top of and outside the roomblock. It appeared that sometime after the rooms had burned and begun to collapse, someone cleared the fallen debris into irregular, drylaid alignments of stone a single course high. The small areas enclosed by the alignments might easily have served as garden plots; certainly no other function was obvious.

The final type of feature found at GC212/212A, and at no other site in the Walhalla Glades, was that of human burials (see Appendix B). Four individuals had been interred at the site, two adult males at GC212 and two adult females at GC212A. Three of the burial pits had been dug through the floors of rooms, and the fourth was in the soil above an outside use surface. It appeared that the interments had been made at or about the same time and were collectively the final event in the history of the site. All the skeletons were accompanied by rather elaborate grave goods ranging from three to eight pottery vessels, including both painted and unpainted types in a variety of vessel forms. The younger of the two females also had a bracelet of shale and turquoise beads around one wrist.

The site configuration data from the A.D. 1100–1150 period are not easy to interpret, but we can offer at least a few possibilities. We have already inferred from the overall decline in the numbers of sites and rooms that fewer people were using or living in the Walhalla Glades after A.D. 1100. A great deal of the decline is accounted for by the almost complete disappearance of one-room sites from the dated sample. This change might mean that agricultural fields were no longer as dispersed as they previously had been, so farmers no longer needed scattered storage rooms or temporary shelters apart from their multiroom habitation and storage complexes. Such an interpretation also fits the apparent increases in average room size and in the proportion of three-room or larger sites in the dated sample. That is, if farming efforts had become more concentrated in a few locations, we might expect that more people were spending more time—perhaps more consecutive summers—and storing larger quantities of food at each site. Consequently, they would have required greater domiciliary and storage space, and room size and numbers would have increased.

Another possibility is that the remaining population lived and farmed more cooperatively than before, with more people perhaps combining their efforts in farming and then storing the harvest communally. This interpretation seems particularly likely with respect to the unusually large sites GC212/212A and GC215. The former was the only excavated site in the Glades that evidenced any length or intensity of use. Its four largest rooms together contained six hearths, and each produced large amounts of artifactual material—pots, manos, metates, and other items—in its burned roof debris. Whether trash or roof assemblages, this material and the hearths reflect a great deal more domiciliary use of this site than is shown by any others excavated, and presumably a relatively large number of people. The accretional growth of roomblock GC212, where the two larger rooms were later additions to the two initially built rooms, further suggests that the trend toward group integration was one that increased through time after A.D. 1100.

Site GC215 on Sky Island also appeared to be the product of communal use by a relatively large group of people. Four of its fifteen excavated rooms had small floor assemblages of pots and grinding tools, but the remainder seemed unlikely to have been used for anything except storage. Given the number of such rooms, we assume that the site was built primarily as a common storage facility by a group of families acting jointly.

Although more people might have been working cooperatively after A.D. 1100, there is no reason to believe that they were engaged in any substantially different activities than before. Agriculture probably remained the focus of the economy, and at least some of the farming was still done in the same kinds of locations as were used during the preceding period. Possibly greater use was made of the lower slopes of the largest drainage, but we have no chronological control over the sites located there. Judging mainly from site GC265, the closest in size of the excavated sites to a "typical" site of this period, there was neither any increase in the number of features inside or outside rooms nor any new kinds of features unknown before A.D. 1100. This stability suggests that subsistence activities remained essentially unchanged, regardless of where or by whom they were performed.

Neither was there any evidence that the plateau was inhabited other than during the summer. Although the relatively large number of hearths at site GC212/212A might have allowed the site to be occupied in winter, there seems to have been no reason for people to remain on the plateau year round. We assume instead that they moved to warmer, lower elevations in the canyon, where exploitable resources were more abundant during the winter months.

Construction Methods

Construction methods between A.D. 1100 and 1150 were remarkably similar to those of the preceding period. The walls of rooms again were built from limestone blocks and slabs, usually laid horizontally on the original ground surface and cemented with adobe mortar. As before, some wall foundations were of large slabs set upright, the more notable examples of this style being the two larger rooms at GC212 and one large room at GC265. Many of the stones, especially in the upper courses, had been shaped by chipping or pecking. The stones were generally aligned evenly on one or both sides of the wall to produce at least one smooth face. Within the standard construction pattern, walls again varied considerably in the size and shape of the stones, the regularity of coursing, and other details.

One difference between the post-A.D. 1100 structures and those of the earlier period was the fairly consistent evidence of full-height masonry walls at the former. Although the wall remains still standing at the time of excavation were no more than a meter high, sufficient fallen rubble was found to have brought the walls up to the roofs at GC212 and GC215 and at the roomblock of GC265. This was not true of GC212A or of the large, noncontiguous room at GC265, where we do not know what kind of superstructure had been present. Still, it

70

seems likely that walls built entirely of stone were standard between A.D. 1100 and 1150.

A construction practice used at least at the two larger excavated sites was the building of groups of rooms all at one time, each group a single structure divided by crosswalls. Three sets of two rooms each had been built in this manner at GC212/212A, as was each entire roomblock at site GC215. Such planned architecture might be taken as further evidence of group coordination of site construction and use after A.D. 1100. At site GC265, the two contiguous rooms excavated apparently had not been built simultaneously, but without excavating the third room in the block, we cannot draw any firm conclusions about the site. Nor can we say with certainty that planned groups of rooms were new to the A.D. 1100–1150 interval. For the preceding period we have only one two-room site, GC408, in which both rooms were excavated, and there a large room had been added onto a smaller one.

Unlike the sites dating between A.D. 1050 and 1100, those of the subsequent period produced evidence of numerous entryways. At GC212 and GC215, five and possibly six above-ground doorways either were visible in the wall fall outside rooms or were indicated by fallen slabs that had probably served as entrance covers. Two possible floor-level doorways, both sealed with rocks and mortar, were also found, one each at GC212 and GC265. A third kind of entryway was indicated in one room each at GC212 and GC215, where shaped slabs of appropriate sizes for roof hatchway covers were found in the fill.

The floors of nearly all the excavated rooms were, as before, simply the natural layer of clay on which the structures were built. Only two rooms with partially slab-paved floors at GC212/212A were exceptions to the rule. The eight hearths found at the dated sites were all circular or oval pits dug into the floors or, in one case, into an outside use surface. They usually were basin shaped in cross section, and they ranged from 55 cm to 1 meter in diameter and from 14 cm to 24 cm deep. Two of the hearths at GC212 were partially lined with small cobbles or slabs (Fig. 23), but all others were completely unlined and unplastered. We assume that the seven fire pits found inside rooms served for heating or cooking or both. The hearth outside roomblock GC212A had the greatest diameter and contained a number of fire-cracked cobbles, suggesting that it might have functioned as a roasting pit.

FIG. 23. Hearth in room 12 at GC212.

Eight rooms at the three excavated sites dating between A.D. 1100 and 1150 produced evidence of roofs constructed from beams and poles and covered with earth. This evidence was found only where the roofs had burned and left chunks of burned adobe, some with beam or pole impressions, charred fragments of wood, and charcoal above the floors of the rooms. Perhaps because of their size, the two larger rooms excavated—those at GC212—each had four corner posts for additional roof support.

AGRICULTURAL FEATURES

The widespread remains of agricultural terraces, garden plots, and check dams form an important part of the archaeology of the Walhalla Glades. Hall (1942:12) first described the variety of agricultural features on the plateau:

Small garden plots are laid out near the houses. The earth appears to have been cleared of rocks, these were thrown or gathered into hillocks or rows separating the strips of ground. Along nearly all practicable contours are terraces, these are sometimes as many as nine deep. They run up to 20 feet wide and 300 yards in length, and may easily be traced.

Several small dams of rock remain in the Walhalla Glades, built across ravines to divert rainwater into ditches which led the water to terraces.

All the agricultural features were visible as drylaid alignments of stone that we referred to as terraces when they paralleled the contours of hillside slopes, as garden plots when they formed rectangular enclosures near habitation sites, and as check dams when they lay across drainages. Three groups of terraces at sites GC268, WP20, and WP53 (Fig. 24) were tested by trenching, and the alignments were found to consist of limestone cobbles and slabs stacked as much as 25 cm or three stones high. They varied widely in their spacing, lying from 75 cm to 5 m apart at the three sites. The tests also showed the accumulated soil behind the terrace alignments to be 15 cm to 25 cm deep. Check dams were built in the same fashion, differing only in their placement across small runoff channels (Fig. 25). Garden plots were exemplified by those already described for site GC212—small, roughly rectangular areas from which rocks had been cleared and arranged in rows outlining the plots.

Our data on the numbers and locations of agricultural features are incomplete because the recording of such sites was not a major focus of the SAR project, nor did Hall assign site numbers to such features during his earlier survey. We can only say that terraces were numerous, garden plots considerably less so, and check dams fairly rare. The recorded locations of terraces and check dams are shown on Map 7, and as mentioned earlier, they tend to coincide with the distribution of habitation/storage sites. The terraces did not seem to be situated with respect to any particular direction or angle of exposure.

Agricultural terraces usually occurred on hillsides that were slightly too steep for natural soil retention, but some were found on nearly level ridgetops where there was no obvious need for erosion control. In fact, one of the more elaborate terrace systems was found near site GC408, where the terrain was fairly level. This variety of placement

FIG. 24. Site WP53, agricultural terraces. Top: view to the north. Bottom: test trench cross-cutting terraces.

FIG. 25. Site WP27, check dam.

suggests that the terraces served several different functions. Some
terrace alignments, for example, were simply ridges of small pebbles
that could easily have been the product of clearing rocks from an area
chosen for planting. Others undoubtedly acted not only to prevent the
erosion of existing soil but also to slow runoff so that new soil could
accumulate. Of course, the retention of runoff water was probably a
primary function of the terraces.

Hall (1942:12) believed that water collected behind check dams was
diverted onto nearby fields through ditches. Although we have no
direct evidence, the locations of several known check dams adjacent to
terrace systems suggest that this diversion system was quite possible.
Another possibility is that soil collected behind the dams was used for
planting in the same fashion as were terraces. Probably because of the
steepness of most of the drainage ravines in the Walhalla Glades,
which would not have lent themselves well to irrigation, known check
dams were few and were located near the heads of the smaller tributary
arroyos.

Terraces located on the steeper hillside slopes made land available for cultivation that otherwise would have been unusable. We do not suppose that terraces were the only areas planted but that any level area where the soil was adequate would also have been cultivated. Yet by accumulating deeper soil and allowing more water to soak into the ground, the terraces might have offered some advantages that other fields could not. These advantages alone might explain the considerable effort that obviously went into the construction of the terrace systems. On the other hand, it could be that the need for additional arable land during a period of population growth demanded the construction of the terraces. We are not certain of the motivating forces behind the terracing activity, but it does demonstrate the crucial role that agriculture played in the prehistoric economy of the Walhalla Glades.

4

Ceramics

A total of 32,507 pottery sherds was collected during survey and excavation in the Walhalla Glades, in addition to 23 whole or partial vessels found as mortuary items in four burials at site GC212/212A. Michael P. Marshall analyzed the ceramic collection, classifying the material, with a few exceptions, according to the ware and type descriptions published by Colton (1952, 1955, 1956, 1958). Marshall also studied a large portion of the collection to isolate any vessel forms that could be identified. As a result, 20 form classes were described on the basis of 126 whole or partially reconstructable vessels.

More than half (55 percent) of the potsherds recovered belonged to the cultural-geographic category known as the Kayenta Branch (Table 6). That is, they consisted of wares generally thought to have been manufactured in northern Arizona east of the Colorado River and associated with what is termed Kayenta Anasazi culture. Among the wares in this group, Tusayan Gray Ware predominated at 31 percent of the entire collection. Its companion painted pottery, Tusayan White Ware, was also relatively abundant and was by far the most common painted ware in the Walhalla Glades. Lesser numbers of Tsegi Orange Ware sherds were found, most of them too eroded to be identified at the type level. Traces of Little Colorado White Ware vessels appeared at the two sites that yielded the largest ceramic collections, GC212/212A and GC215. Presumably these types were rare because they were

TABLE 6.
Pottery sherds in the Walhalla Plateau collection.

	Number	Percent of Total
KAYENTA BRANCH	17,776	54.7
Tusayan Gray Ware	10,079	31.0
Kana'a Gray	2	
Coconino Gray	77	
Medicine Gray	5	
O'Leary Tooled	2	
Tusayan Plain	788	
Tusayan Corrugated	6,070	
Moenkopi Corrugated	2,729	
Unidentified	406	
Tusayan White Ware	5,617	17.3
Black Mesa B/W	126	
Sosi B/W	353	
Dogoszhi B/W	255	
Flagstaff B/W	237	
Shato B/W	8	
Unidentified	4,638	
Tsegi Orange Ware	1,853	5.7
Medicine B/R	44	
Tusayan B/R	85	
Cameron Polychrome	58	
Citadel Polychrome	133	
Unidentified	1,533	
Little Colorado White Ware	227	0.7
Holbrook B/W	54	
Walnut B/W	3	
Padre B/W	3	
Unidentified	167	
VIRGIN BRANCH	12,466	38.3
Walhalla Gray Ware	6,150	18.9
Walhalla Plain	1,444	
Walhalla Corrugated	4,706	

TABLE 6 *(continued)*.

	Number	Percent of Total
Walhalla White Ware	649	2.0
Walhalla B/W		
Black Mesa style	41	
Sosi-Dogoszhi style	556	
Unidentified style	51	
Shinarump Gray Ware	5,176	15.9
Shinarump Brown	738	
Shinarump Corrugated	4,438	
Shinarump White Ware	477	1.5
Virgin B/W		
Sosi-Dogoszhi style	465	
Unidentified style	12	
Logandale Gray Ware	5	Trace
Logandale Corrugated	5	
Moapa Gray Ware	9	Trace
KAYENTA OR VIRGIN BRANCH	540	1.7
San Juan Red Ware	540	1.7
Deadmans B/R	109	
Middleton Red	241	
Middleton B/R	155	
Middleton Polychrome	35	
COHONINA BRANCH	1,164	3.6
San Francisco Mountain Gray Ware	1,164	3.6
Floyd Gray	6	
Deadmans Gray ·	1,043	
Deadmans Fugitive Red	115	
UNIDENTIFIED	561	1.7
TOTAL	32,507	

imported over a fairly great distance from the lower Little Colorado River area.

Next most abundant (38 percent) were sherds belonging to the Virgin Branch of northern Arizona and southern Utah west of the Colorado River. Most of these sherds belonged to one of two unpainted gray-paste wares, Shinarump Gray Ware and Walhalla Gray Ware. The latter was named and described by Marshall (1979), who first recognized it among the pottery from the Walhalla Glades. The painted wares of the Virgin Branch, Shinarump White Ware and Walhalla White Ware, appeared only in small quantities in the collection. When the decorative styles on these sherds could be identified, they were either the Black Mesa, the Sosi, or the Dogoszhi style, all adopted from Tusayan White Ware. The Flagstaff design style was absent. One vessel each of Logandale Gray Ware and Moapa Gray Ware, whose distribution was centered farther to the west in northern Arizona, indicated that trade with those areas was probably minimal.

San Juan Red Ware made up a minor percentage of the collection from the Walhalla Glades, as it seems to do throughout northern Arizona. Its exact center of manufacture is not known, and we hesitate to assign it to either the Kayenta or Virgin cultural branches. The final ware represented was San Francisco Mountain Gray Ware. Although not an abundant member of the collection (3.6 percent), it still was surprisingly common given its association with the Cohonina Branch south of the Colorado River. From this ware's presence we surmise that more trade goods were brought across the river from the south than we had originally expected.

The pottery types represented in each ware and their quantities are listed in Table 6. For all sites that yielded ceramics, the ware and type occurrences can be found in Tables 7 and 8.

VESSEL FORMS

The sherds recovered from rooms 9, 11, 12, 22, 34, 39A, and 39B at site GC212/212A and from all the excavated rooms at site GC215 were examined for reconstructable vessel forms. These proveniences were chosen because they were known to contain relatively large numbers of broken vessels and because proveniences outside rooms tended to contain highly fragmented trash in which few reconstructable pots could be recognized. Within the sample, 103 vessels were present in portions large enough—up to three-quarters complete—to allow their forms to be reconstructed. Adding the vessels recovered from burials brought the total to 126.

Twenty form categories were defined by Michael P. Marshall on the basis of this sample, including seven bowl and thirteen jar forms. These are illustrated schematically in Fig. 26 and described in the following list.

Vessel Forms Identified Among the Walhalla Glades Ceramics

Note: All diameters are from measurable specimens, not necessarily all specimens in a type, and refer to diameter at the vessel mouth. Further measurements of specimens of some types can be found in Table 10. For illustrations, see Fig. 26.

1. Small hemispherical bowl with direct rim. Type 1a has horizontal loop handles on exterior below rim. Diameter 9.4–13.5 cm.

2. Medium-sized hemispherical bowl with direct rim. Diameter 14.0–17.0 cm.

3. Large hemispherical bowl with direct rim. Diameter 18.0–27.0 cm.

4. Large, shallow (less than hemispherical) bowl with direct or flared (type 4a) rim. Diameter 23.3 cm.

5. Large hemispherical bowl with flared rim. Diameter 26.6 cm.

6. Biconcave bowl with direct rim. Diameter 16.0 cm.

7. Ladle with hemispherical bowl, direct rim, and coil handle. Bowl diameters 10.7 cm and 11.0 cm.

8. Small jar (mug) with vertical loop handle and direct or flared rim. Diameters 6.4 cm and 8.0 cm.

9. Small or medium-sized wide-mouthed jar with vertical (common) or horizontal (rare) loop handle. Type 9 has an ovoid body, type 9a a globular body. Diameter 8.0–12.0 cm.

TABLE 7.
Pottery sherds from Walhalla Glades sites with more than 100 sherds.[1]

	Pre-1050	1050–1100									1100–1150			
	GC 270	GC 268	GC 309	GC 329B	GC 378	GC 408	GC 414A	WP 14	WP 72	GC² 212	GC² 212A	GC² 215	GC 265
Tusayan Gray Ware	40	119	23	104	71	279	45	105	83	5,694	217	2,899	133
Kana'a Gray	1												1
Coconino Gray	1	2		5			4	2		52	2		
Medicine Gray	1									4			
O'Leary Tooled										1	1		
Tusayan Plain	9	18	1	44	14	28	2	2		574	29	24	1
Tusayan Corrugated	28	83	16	53	57	251*	34	98†	82‡	3,269	114	1,833	12
Moenkopi Corrugated			1	2						1,449	67	1,039	112§
Unidentified		16	5				5	3	1	345	4	3	7
Tusayan White Ware	21	55	17	22	34	67	62	17	3	4,093	245	831	25
Black Mesa B/W	1	7		7	7	3	27	7		59	15	1	
Sosi B/W		1	8	11	6	6				178	3	113	2
Dogoszhi B/W		1		4				4		136	47	99	3
Flagstaff B/W										118		56	3
Shato B/W										5	3		
Unidentified	20	46	9		21	58	35‖	6	3	3,597	177	562	17
Tsegi Orange Ware		32	33	1	17	24	2	4	3	1,380	160	169	8
Medicine B/R		1								41		1	

	1	2	3	4	5	6	7	8	9	10	11	12	13
Tusayan B/R	2									69	5	7	6
Cameron Poly	30		33#							54	3	1	2
Citadel Poly										18	41	35	
Unidentified										1,198	111	125	
San Juan Red Ware	5					19				311	109	63	18
Deadmans B/R	3									95	1		
Middleton Red	2		—							129	15		
Middleton B/R						19**				67	78	63	8
Middleton Poly										20	15		10
Little Colorado White Ware						40				31	17	139	
Holbrook B/W										31	17	6	
Walnut B/W												3	
Padre B/W												3	
Unidentified						40††						127	
Walhalla Gray Ware	5	11	87	62	22	157	127	4	165	3,017	446	1,605	246
Walhalla Plain	1	4	2	25	5	10	6	1	8	566	153	584	23
Walhalla Corrugated	4	7	85	37	17	147	121‡‡	3	157§§	2,451	293	1,021	223‖
Walhalla White Ware	9	8	1	1	12	73	1	1		326	125	70	6
Walhalla B/W													
Black Mesa style						41##							
Sosi-Dogoszhi style		6				5							6
Unidentified style	9	2			12	27		12		326	125	70	6

TABLE 7 (continued).

	Pre-1050	1050–1100								1100–1150			
	GC 270	GC 268	GC 309	GC 329B	GC 378	GC 408	GC 414A	WP 14	WP 72	GC² 212	GC² 212A	GC² 215	GC 265
Shinarump Gray Ware	5			30	53	85				1,667	28	3,220	
Shinarump Brown	4				1	2				491	4	219	
Shinarump Corrugated	1			30***	52	83†††				1,176	24	3,001	
Shinarump White Ware					4	6				269	64	126	4
Virgin B/W													
Sosi-Dogoszhi style													
Unidentified style					4	6				269	64	126	4
San Francisco Mountain Gray Ware	43	36						5		651	49	335	1
Floyd Gray	1			6	1	6				3			

84

Deadmans Gray	39	32	6	1	6		5		633	47	254	1
Deadmans Fugitive Red	3	4							15	2	81	
Other Wares												
Logandale Corrugated									5			
Moapa Gray Ware											9	
Unidentified	2	1		5	35				455	15	46	
TOTAL	127	259	168	228	223	751	277	136	254	17,899	1,475	9,512	441

¹Includes only those "GC-" sites that were tested or excavated by the School of American Research. Ceramics from Hall's 1939 survey collections are included in these counts.

²Clusters of sherds belonging to single vessels were present at sites GC212, GC212A, and GC215 but were too numerous to be noted on this table.

*At least 117 sherds belong to 2 vessels.
†Probably only a few vessels.
‡Probably one or a few vessels.
§At least 88 sherds belong to 1 vessel.
‖At least 23 sherds belong to 2 vessels.
#One vessel.
**Fourteen sherds belong to one vessel.

††One vessel.
‡‡At least 101 sherds belong to one vessel.
§§143 sherds belong to one vessel.
‖‖At least 86 sherds belong to 1 vessel.
##One vessel.
***Probably belong to two vessels.
†††At least 48 sherds belong to 1 vessel.

TABLE 8.
Pottery sherds from Walhalla Plateau sites
with fewer than 100 sherds.

	WP 5	WP 22	WP 24	WP 34	WP 36	WP 37	WP 41	WP 46	WP 53
Tusayan Gray Ware	3	13	17	20	2	17	3	10	5
Kana'a Gray									
Coconino Gray									1
Tusayan Plain	3	2			2	1			3
Tusayan Corrugated		9	13	14		15	3		1
Moenkopi Corrugated				4				10	
Unidentified		2	4	2		1			
Tusayan White Ware		8	12	8	4	16	3	2	1
Black Mesa B/W						4			1
Sosi B/W						1	1		
Dogoszhi B/W			1			4			
Flagstaff B/W						1			
Unidentified		8	11	8	4	6	2	2	
Tsegi Orange Ware	2		3	1		2			
Medicine B/R	1								
Tusayan B/R			2			1			
Unidentified	1		1	1		1			
San Juan Red Ware			1			3			
Deadmans B/R						2			
Middleton Red			1			1			
Walhalla Gray Ware	5	2	22		6	19		9	2
Walhalla Plain	2	2	5		1	8			1
Walhalla Corrugated	3		17		5	11		9	1
Walhalla White Ware			3		1	2			
Walhalla B/W									
Sosi-Dogoszhi style			3			2			
Unidentified style					1				
Shinarump Gray Ware	3				11	20			
Shinarump Brown	2				11	1			

WP 55	WP 56	WP 61	WP 62	WP 67	WP 78	WP 79	Other WP Sites*	GC 264	GC 276	GC 326	KP 1	WT 2	WT 8	WT 10
8	6	16	8	3	22		14	25	21	13		26**		15
										1				
		1							6					
		3	1	2					15	10				
7	6	9	5	2	19		10	25		2				
1			3				2					26**		15
		3			1		2							
2	9	5	18	4	7		4	10	6	4	2			
	2													
					7			3	1					
	5		7											
2	2	5	11	4			4	7	5	4	2			
		1			1	2				8				
		1			1	2				8				
			1							2				
										2				
			1											
11	22	3	13	2	4	6	5	25	15	20	5			
1	8		3	2	2				1	18	2			
10	14	3	10		2	6	5	25	14	2	3			
			1			2		3			5			
			1			2		3			5			
					1					1	36	13**		3
					1					1				1

87

TABLE 8 *(continued)*.

	WP 5	*WP 22*	*WP 24*	*WP 34*	*WP 36*	*WP 37*	*WP 41*	*WP 46*	*WP 53*
Shinarump Corrugated	1					19			
Shinarump White Ware									
Virgin B/W									
Sosi style									
Unidentified style									
San Francisco Mountain Gray Ware		5		2				2	
Floyd Gray									
Deadmans Gray		5		2				2	
Deadmans Fugitive Red									
Unidentified									
TOTAL	13	28	58	31	24	79	6	23	8

*Includes sites with 3 sherds or fewer: WP6, WP12, WP15, WP17, WP18, WP30, WP38, WP40, WP50, WP58, WP63, and WP66.
**One vessel.

10. Small, wide-mouthed, low globular jar with flared rim and no handle. Diameter 8.8 cm.

11. Medium-sized or large, wide-mouthed, low globular jar with lugs. Diameter estimated between 15 and 20 cm.

12. Medium-sized, wide-mouthed, globular jar with constricted neck and flared rim. Diameter 12.0 cm.

13. Medium-sized wide-mouthed jar with flared rim. Type 13 has an ovoid body, type 13a a globular body. Diameter 10.0–17.5 cm.

14. Large wide-mouthed jar with flared rim. Type 14a has an ovoid body, type 14b a globular body, and type 14 an indeterminable body shape. Diameter 18.0–24.0 cm.

15. Small or medium-sized narrow-mouthed jar with direct or flared rim. Diameters 8.0 and 9.0 cm.

WP 55	WP 56	WP 61	WP 62	WP 67	WP 78	WP 79	Other WP Sites*	GC 264	GC 276	GC 326	KP 1	WT 2	WT 8	WT 10
											36		13**	2
					2			2						
								2						
					2									
		1		2			1		14	2	2			
										2				
		1		2			1		5			1		
									9			1		
									2					
21	38	25	41	12	38	8	24	65	59	49	50	26	13	18

16. Large narrow-mouthed jar with direct or flared rim. Diameters 10.0 and 11.0 cm.

17. Canteens: jars with very narrow mouths, with or without lugs. Diameters 2.7, 3.0, and 3.5 cm. One boat-shaped.

18. Large, globular, neckless jars. No measurements.

19. Seed jars: low, globular, neckless jars. Diameters 7.0, 7.3, and 11.0 cm.

20. Medium-sized, globular, wide-mouthed jar with flared rim and four bulbous projections on body. Diameter 8.4 cm.

Jars were more numerous and diverse in form than were bowls in the sample, though we cannot say whether this was true of the collection as a whole. Large wide-mouthed jars without handles (form 14) appeared most frequently (Table 9), followed by identical but smaller

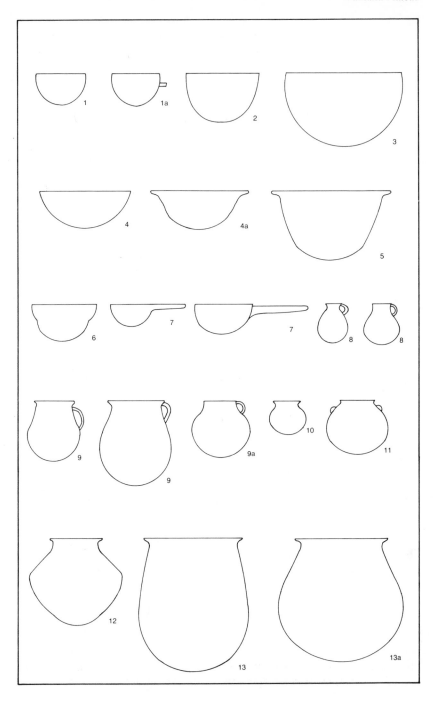

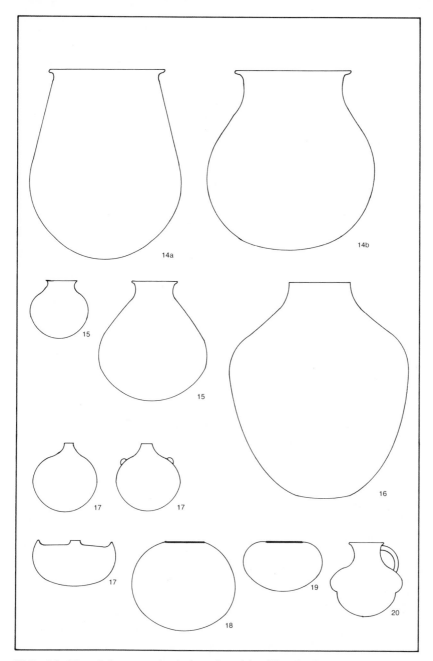

FIG. 26. Vessel forms and relative sizes identified in the Walhalla Glades ceramics. Numbers are those of the types listed in the text.

TABLE 9.
Reconstructable vessel forms.

	BOWL TYPES								
	1	1a	2	3	4	4a	5	6	7
UNPAINTED POTTERY									
Tusayan Plain									
Tusayan Corrugated									
Moenkopi Corrugated									
Walhalla Plain									
Walhalla Corrugated									
Shinarump Brown			1						
Shinarump Corrugated			1	1					
Deadmans Gray									
Moapa Corrugated									
Unidentified Gray Ware									
PAINTED POTTERY									
Black Mesa B/W								1	
Sosi B/W									
Dogoszhi B/W									
Flagstaff B/W		1	1	4			1		1
Tusayan White Ware			1	1					
Tusayan B/R				1					
Cameron Polychrome				1					
Citadel Polychrome				1					
Cameron or Citadel Poly				1					
Tsegi Orange Ware			1						
Holbrook B/W	2								1
Walnut B/W	1		1						
Little Colorado White Ware				2					
Walhalla B/W				6	1				
Virgin B/W	1			2					
Deadmans B/R									
Middleton Red				1					
Middleton B/R				4					
Middleton Polychrome				1					
Unidentified White Ware						1			
TOTAL	4	1	6	26	1	1	1	1	2

						JAR TYPES											
8	9	9a	10	11	12	13	13a	14	14a	14b	15	16	17	18	19	20	TOTAL
												1					1
1	1					1		3	2								8
						1	1	9	1	2							14
												1		5			6
	2	2				1		9		2		1					17
												1	2				4
	2	2				1	2	7	2	1	1	1					20
								1				1					2
							1										1
											1						1
																	1
1																	1
1																	1
																	8
															1	1	4
			1		1												3
																	1
																	1
																	1
																	1
																	3
															1		3
																	2
				1													8
													1				4
															1		1
																	1
																	4
																	1
															1		2
3	5	4	1	1	1	4	4	29	5	5	2	6	3	5	4	1	126

jars (form 13) and small or medium-sized pitchers with handles (forms 8 and 9). More specialized jar forms included three canteens and four seed jars, so called because their forms suggested that they had served such purposes. Nearly half (47 percent) of the jars exhibited carbonization on their bases and body sherds, indicating that they had been used in cooking.

Among the bowl forms, large hemispherical vessels (form 3) were by far the most numerous, again followed by forms differing only in size. All other bowls were represented by only one or two specimens each. None of the bowls had been charred before breakage.

A few jar forms occurred mainly or exclusively among the painted pottery types (Fig. 27)—for example, seed jars, small pitchers, and squat, globular jars with constricted necks. Most jars, however, were unpainted gray ware vessels (Figs. 28 and 29), as might be expected on the assumption that such pots were used primarily in cooking and storage. Conversely, bowls were almost always painted types of white or red wares. The three exceptions were all Shinarump Gray Ware bowls.

FIG. 27. Tusayan Black-on-red jar. (Scale is 16 cm long.)

FIG. 28. Shinarump Corrugated jar from site GC215. (Scale is 16 cm long.)

Of the pottery types in the sample that were represented by more than one or two specimens, most occurred in a variety of forms. A few seemed to be more specialized. Five of the six Walhalla Plain vessels were large, globular, neckless jars, and no other types appeared in this form. Another example is the occurrence of all the Middleton types of San Juan Red Ware as large, hemispherical bowls. Such apparent form specialization is difficult to interpret, especially when indicated by so few specimens, but it does raise the possibility that some kinds of pottery were manufactured only for particular purposes or were imported selectively in particular forms.

MORTUARY ASSEMBLAGES

The 23 whole or partial vessels recovered from burials provided further information on vessel forms, sizes, and decorative designs (Figs. 30–33). For descriptions of the ways in which these pots were

FIG. 29. Two small jars from site GC408. Left: Walhalla Plain. Right:
Tusayan Corrugated. (Scale is 16 cm long.)

arranged in the burials, see Appendix B. The types identified in each
assemblage and their dimensions are listed in Table 10.

The mortuary assemblages consisted overwhelmingly of painted pottery. Of the 23 vessels, 18 belonged to one of the five white or red
wares represented—Tusayan White Ware, Little Colorado White Ware,
Tsegi Orange Ware, Walhalla White Ware, and Shinarump White
Ware. This generalization was true of jars as well as bowls, even
though in the larger sample, jars usually were gray ware vessels. Seven
of the twelve jars in the mortuary group were painted types, the others
belonging to the more common utility types, Tusayan Corrugated,
Walhalla Corrugated, and Shinarump Corrugated.

A great diversity of types was represented, including all the major
painted and corrugated types of the A.D. 1100–1150 time period. If
any preference for a particular decorative style existed, it was for the
Flagstaff design style as seen on Flagstaff Black-on-white and Walnut
Black-on-white. The range of forms was as diverse as the types present, but overall the assemblages were almost evenly divided between

FIG. 30. Pots found with burial 18 at GC212. From left: Citadel Polychrome, Shinarump Corrugated, Tusayan Black-on-red, Tusayan
White Ware, Walhalla Black-on-white. (Scale is 16 cm long.)

FIG. 31. Pots found with burial 25 at GC212. From left: Walhalla Corrugated, Walhalla Black-on-white, Flagstaff Black-on-white. (Scale is
16 cm long.)

97

FIG. 32. Pots found with burial 46 at GC212A. From left: Dogoszhi Black-on-white, Tusayan Corrugated, Walnut Black-on-white, Tusayan Black-on-red, Flagstaff Black-on-white, Sosi Black-on-white, Flagstaff Black-on-white. A second Walnut Black-on-white bowl and a partial Shinarump Corrugated jar are not shown. (Scale is 16 cm long.)

FIG. 33. Pots found with burial 53 at GC212A. From left: Flagstaff Black-on-white, Walnut Black-on-white, Walhalla Corrugated, Holbrook Black-on-white, Virgin Black-on-white. (Scale is 16 cm long.)

TABLE 10.
Pottery vessels found in mortuary assemblages.

	Form	Form Category	Diameter at Mouth (cm)	Maximum Diameter (cm)	Height (cm)
Burial GC212-18					
Tusayan White Ware	jar	20	8.4	18.5	16.8
Tusayan B/R	jar	12	12.0	26.0	20.0
Cameron or Citadel Polychrome (partial vessel)	bowl	3	21.5		12.0
Walhalla B/W	bowl	4	23.3		10.2
Shinarump Corrugated	jar	9	10.5	14.0	14.5
Burial GC212-25					
Flagstaff B/W	ladle	7	8.3–10.7		5.8
Walhalla B/W	bowl	3	18.3		10.0
Walhalla Corrugated	jar	9a	8.0		11.2
Middleton Polychrome (large sherd)	bowl	3	27.0		
Burial GC212A-46					
Sosi B/W	jar	8	6.4	8.7	10.1
Dogoszhi B/W	jar	8	6.4	13.0	11.3
Flagstaff B/W	bowl	5	26.6		15.3
Flagstaff B/W	bowl	1	10.2–11.5		7.1
Walnut B/W	bowl	2	17.0		12.5
Walnut B/W	bowl	1	13.5		6.9
Tusayan B/R	jar	10	8.8	17.0	13.0
Tusayan Corrugated	jar	8	8.0		13.5
Shinarump Corrugated (partial vessel)	jar	13a			
Burial GC212A-53					
Flagstaff B/W	bowl	2	15.4		11.0
Holbrook B/W	bowl	1	9.4		4.8
Walnut B/W	seed jar	19	7.3	19.0	10.5
Virgin B/W	canteen	17	3.0	19.0	16.0
Walhalla Corrugated	jar	9	11.5	19.0	21.0

jars and bowls. We interpret the variety of forms in each burial assemblage as approximating the combination of vessels required for use in most everyday activities. Some vessels, such as the unique Tusayan White Ware jar (form 20) in burial 18, might have been prized personal possessions of the deceased.

CHANGES THROUGH TIME

That certain pottery types appeared, reached their maximum abundance, declined, and became extinct at fairly well-established times allowed us to date some of the sites in the Walhalla Glades, as discussed in Chapter 3. These "index fossils" were chiefly the painted types of Tusayan White Ware and Tsegi Orange Ware. Having arranged the sites in chronological order, we then examined the behavior through time of other wares and types that were not as useful in the dating process. Total sherd counts by type for the two major periods of settlement—A.D. 1050–1100 and 1100–1150—are given in Table 11. For contrast, we have listed separately in the table the type distributions for site GC270, which may have dated slightly before A.D. 1050, and for a group of sites dated by Marshall between A.D. 950 and 1050 on the basis of their small surface collections.

Within Tusayan Gray Ware, two main trends can be seen in Table 11. First, Tusayan Plain decreased through time, making up 59 percent of the ware in the earliest group, 17 percent in the A.D. 1050–1100 sample, and only 7 percent after A.D. 1100. Although Tusayan Plain is not a type per se but simply a sorting category for any uncorrugated body sherds of Tusayan Gray Ware, this decline does correspond to the known trend within the ware for smooth-surfaced vessels to be replaced by corrugated ones between about A.D. 800 and 1100. After A.D. 1100, the trend began to reverse, as is reflected in the Walhalla Glades pottery by the increase of Moenkopi Corrugated, with its flattened coils, at the expense of Tusayan Corrugated in the later sample.

The Tusayan Gray Ware percentage remained fairly stable between A.D. 1050 and 1150, though it may have declined somewhat from a higher percentage before A.D. 1050. The two major wares of the Virgin Branch, however, did apparently change in frequency relative to one another. Walhalla Gray Ware was present in fairly large amounts (26 percent) in the presumably early group, remained constant until A.D.

TABLE 11.
Distribution of pottery types through time.

	A.D. 950–1050*		GC270		A.D. 1050–1100**		A.D. 1100–1050***	
	No.	%	No.	%	No.	%	No.	%
Tusayan Gray Ware	112	48.5	40	31.5	641	33.6	8,943	30.5
Kana'a Gray	8		1					
Coconino Gray	8		1		11		55	
Medicine Gray	2		1				4	
O'Leary Tooled							2	
Tusayan Plain	66		9		107		628	
Tusayan Corrugated	23		28		494		5,228	
Moenkopi Corrugated					1		2,667	
Unidentified	5				28		359	
Tusayan White Ware	25	10.8	21	16.5	257	13.5	5,194	17.7
Kana'a B/W	4							
Black Mesa B/W	16		1		51		60	
Sosi B/W					32		308	
Dogoszhi B/W					5		241	
Flagstaff B/W							224	
Shato B/W							8	
Unidentified	5		20		169		4,353	
Tsegi Orange Ware					109	5.7	1,717	5.8
Medicine B/R					1		42	
Tusayan B/R					1		81	

TABLE 11 (continued).

	A.D. 950–1050*		GC270		A.D. 1050–1100**		A.D. 1100–1050***	
	No.	%	No.	%	No.	%	No.	%
Cameron Polychrome							58	
Citadel Polychrome					33†		100	
Unidentified					74		1,436	
San Juan Red Ware	12	5.2	2	1.6	30	1.6	501	1.7
Deadmans B/R	12				9		96	
Middleton Red			2		21		215	
Middleton B/R							155	
Middleton Polychrome							35	
Walhalla Gray Ware	60	26.0	5	3.9	466	24.4	5,314	18.1
Walhalla Plain	41		1		52		1,326	
Walhalla Corrugated	19		4		414		3,988	
Walhalla White Ware			9	7.1	95	5.0	527	1.8
Shinarump Gray Ware	6	2.6	5	3.9	168	8.8	4,915	16.8
Shinarump Brown	1		4		3		714	
Shinarump Corrugated	5		1		165		4,201	

Ware	n	%	n	%	n	%	n	%
Shinarump White Ware	16	6.9			10	0.5	463	1.6
San Francisco Mountain Gray Ware			43	33.8	49	2.6	1,036	3.5
Floyd Gray	16		1				3	
Deadmans Gray			39		45		935	
Deadmans Fugitive Red			3		4		98	
Little Colorado White Ware					40†	2.1	187	0.6
Holbrook B/W							54	
Walnut B/W							3	
Padre B/W							3	
Unidentified					40		127	
Other								
Logandale Corrugated							5	
Moapa Gray Ware							9	
Unidentified			2		41		516	
TOTAL	231		127		1,906		29,327	

*Includes sites GC332, GC339, GC376, GC381, GC398A, and GC425. Classification based on Marshall's examination of Hall's survey collections; no new collections made by SAR.

**Includes sites GC268, GC309, GC329B, GC378, GC408, and GC414A, all tested or excavated by SAR.

***Includes sites GC212 and 212A, GC215, and GC265, all tested or excavated by SAR.

†One vessel.

1100, and then declined to 18 percent of the sample. Shinarump Gray Ware showed the opposite pattern: it was present in small amounts in the two earliest periods, but almost equaled Walhalla Gray Ware between A.D. 1100 and 1150. Walhalla and Shinarump white wares paralleled the gray wares in decline or increase, though the changes in percentage were never great.

This reciprocal pattern between the Walhalla and Shinarump wares is difficult to interpret in view of our earlier opinion (Schwartz, Chapman, and Kepp 1980) that Walhalla material was largely indigenous to the plateau and Shinarump pottery to the Grand Canyon. It is hard to imagine that many large Shinarump Gray Ware jars—the form in which that ware most often appeared—were carried up from the canyon to the plateau, though perhaps this was the case. Alternatively, and more plausibly, some of the pottery we recognize as Shinarump may also have been manufactured in the Walhalla Glades.

In either case, the two Virgin Branch gray wares together equaled Tusayan Gray Ware in abundance during both major periods of settlement in the Walhalla Glades. Such proportions were not unexpected, given the peripheral location of the plateau to both the Kayenta Branch and the Virgin Branch. The equal percentages make it difficult to assign the settlement to one branch or the other, but we believe that our earlier generalization (Schwartz, Chapman, and Kepp 1980) about the cultural affiliation of the Grand Canyon inhabitants holds true here as well. That is, these people were originally of Kayenta Branch affiliation, but upon moving into new territory around the Grand Canyon, they began to manufacture slightly different pottery of locally available materials—pottery still within the Kayenta Branch tradition but recognized archaeologically as Virgin Branch wares.

We suspect further that some ceramics classified as Kayenta were also produced locally because large Moenkopi Corrugated jars, for example, were probably no more likely to be imported over long distances than were large Shinarump Corrugated vessels. Wherever the different types of vessels were produced, it seems clear that the prehistoric inhabitants of the Walhalla Glades were offshoots of the Kayenta ceramic tradition who developed through time somewhat different characteristics that have come to be diagnostic of Virgin Branch culture.

104

5

Stone Artifacts

The stone artifacts collected during survey and excavation in the Walhalla Glades totaled 11,971, the bulk of them coming from the large sites GC212/212A and GC215. Of the entire collection, 11,469 (96 percent) had been manufactured by chipping and only 491 (4 percent) by grinding or a combination of chipping and grinding. Eleven pieces were largely unmodified stones not assigned to either major category. Even when the large quantity of unused waste flakes among the chipped stone artifacts is excluded from these figures, ground stone implements make up only 9 percent of the collection.

This great disparity between the sizes of the chipped and ground stone inventories probably reflects the different modes of manufacture and use rather than the relative importance of any activities performed with the tools. Most chipped stone implements were made simply by knocking a flake from a core and using it once or a few times without any further modification, although occasionally a few retouch flakes were removed to shape the tool. Ground stone tools, on the other hand, usually required greater preparation and were designed to be used for long periods of time until they were too worn to function well; manos and metates are prime examples of such artifacts. Consequently, it was not surprising to find a great preponderance of chipped stone artifacts relative to those of ground stone in the lithic collection.

With the exception of a few Basketmaker projectile points from the vicinity of Greenland Lake, the kinds of stone tools found in survey and excavation in the Walhalla Glades were generally typical of those from Pueblo sites in northern Arizona. The kinds of implements identified were used for a range of activities including hunting, woodworking, probably hide processing, the grinding of corn and perhaps nuts and seeds, and pottery manufacture.

CHIPPED STONE ARTIFACTS

The chipped stone artifacts from the Walhalla Plateau were classified and described by Chapman in 1971 (see Appendix C, where the artifacts are illustrated). More than half of this category (57 percent) consisted of unused debitage and spent cores, the by-products of tool manufacture (Table 12). Flakes resulting from decortication and trimming during core preparation made up most of the debitage. Another 32 percent of the chipped stone artifacts were chert flakes that had been used as tools without any retouch modification, and only 11 percent (1,234 specimens) had been further modified after removal from the core. Most of the modified tools exhibited retouch flaking along only their working edges, as if the overall shape of the implement was already suitable or perhaps mattered little. Only 291 chipped stone tools could be called "refined" artifacts, that is, they were bifacially flaked over all or much of their surfaces to produce a desired form. These specimens included large and small projectile points, knives, and other implements whose functions could not be determined (Table 13). Judging from the evidence of wear patterns, the marginally retouched flakes had been used as gouges, drills, gravers, scrapers, and knives (Table 14).

There was a certain conservative tendency for the marginally retouched flakes (and probably the utilized flakes as well) to be used for two or three different purposes. Forty-two percent of the marginally retouched tools had multiple working edges that combined the functions of scrapers, gouges, and knives. A total of 1,754 such use edges was recognized on 943 artifacts, giving an average of 1.8 working edges per flake. This multifunctionality makes sense because many tasks undoubtedly required a variety of operations, and it would simply have been more efficient to reuse a flake already in hand than to manufacture a new one for each new operation.

The raw material most commonly used for chipped stone tools was

106

TABLE 12.
Distribution of major categories of chipped
stone artifacts.

	Cores	Debitage	Utilized Flakes	Marginally Retouched Artifacts	Bifacially Retouched Artifacts	Total
Pre-A.D. 1050?						
GC270	2	15	19	7	1	44
A.D. 1050–1100						
GC268	4	40	47	14	12	117
GC309		2	1			3
GC329B	2	16	8	2	1	29
GC378	1	59	95	13	4	172
GC408	1	79	27	8	3	118
GC414A		15	10	2		27
Subtotal	8	211	188	39	20	466
Percent	1.7	45.3	40.3	8.4	4.3	
A.D. 1100–1150						
GC212	95	4,597	2,078	471	168	7,409
GC212A	4	59	55	5	2	125
GC215	5	1,246	874	298	30	2,453
GC265		4	6	1		11
Subtotal	104	5,906	3,013	775	200	9,988
Percent	1.0	59.1	30.2	7.8	2.0	
Post-A.D. 1050						
GC264		1				1
WP14		15	18	3		36
WP24	1	20	23	5	2	51
WP37		8	12	2	1	23
WP46			1			1
WP72		5	7	1	4	17
Undated Sites						
GC276		25	23	10	8	66
WP2					3	3
WP5	3	224	239	58	32	556
WP6		7	2	3		12
WP12		1	2			3

TABLE 12 *(continued)*.

	Cores	Debitage	Utilized Flakes	Marginally Retouched Artifacts	Bifacially Retouched Artifacts	Total
WP13		3	9			12
WP22		10	38	25	3	76
WP36		3	13	1	1	18
WP40		2	1	1		4
WP41		2	1			3
WP53	1		1	1		3
WP58		2	1			3
WP67			3			3
WP70		1	1		1	3
WP71	1	5	8	2	1	17
KP1		6	1	2		9
WT1			4	2	1	7
WT10				2	5	7
Other Sites*	1	5	9	4	8	27
TOTAL	121	6,477	3,637	943	291	11,469
PERCENT	1.0	56.5	31.7	8.2	2.5	

*Includes sites with only 1 or 2 artifacts: WP3, WP4, WP18, WP20, WP21, WP23, WP25, WP29, WP30, WP31, WP44, WP47, WP51, WP57, WP60, WP61, WP65, WP66, WP73, WP77, WT2, and one provenience unknown.

the locally abundant Kaibab chert, from which was made 89 percent of the marginally retouched implements and 51 percent of the bifacially retouched artifacts. Beds of both tabular and nodular chert were exposed in the sides of drainages and outcropped on the ridgetops of the Walhalla Glades. However, not all Kaibab chert appeared suitable for use in tool manufacture. The tabular outcroppings were often laced with fractures that rendered them unusable, and much of the nodular chert was extremely soft and grainy. In fact, no sources of Kaibab chert suitable for use were located during the SAR survey, though the preponderance of this material among the chipped stone artifacts indicated that such sources did exist.

Nearly all the Kaibab chert used in manufacture in the Walhalla Glades was of the nodular variety, with a grainy cortex 2–10 mm thick surrounding an inner core of much finer crystalline structure. In color, Kaibab chert is predominately white or light gray but also yellow-brown, gray-green, pink, and red. The texture of the material used for tools covered the full range from soft and grainy to brittle and glassy.

At least two varieties of chert that do not occur in the Kaibab formation were also used in tool manufacture. Only 10 percent of the marginally retouched implements consisted of these exotic cherts, but 38 percent of the bifacially flaked tools were made from them. One variety ranged from orange to dark red in color, the other from light gray to dark gray, and both were even-textured and nearly glassy. Although some debitage and one core of exotic chert were found, the appearance of only a few decortication flakes suggested that these materials were imported as prepared cores or perhaps in some cases as finished tools. Presumably the exotic materials were used so extensively in bifacially retouched artifacts because they were of better quality than the local Kaibab chert.

Another kind of exotic chert, chalcedony, was distinguished as a separate type of raw material in this study. Chalcedony included a great variety of glassy, nearly transparent cherts but did not appear in great quantity. Chalcedony too was used mainly in the production of bifacially retouched tools (8 percent of such artifacts), and it made up less than 1 percent of the marginally retouched implements. Finally, nine bifaces had been manufactured from obsidian, another exotic material whose exact source area is unknown.

GROUND STONE ARTIFACTS

Theodore R. Reinhart classified and described the ground stone artifacts of the Walhalla Glades in 1969 (see Appendix D). The most numerous types were beads and pendants, but this representation was entirely due to the discovery of 166 such ornaments as part of a single bracelet in a burial at site GC212A. If these artifacts are treated as a single specimen, then the composition of the ground stone collection is predominately grinding tools, with manos (46 percent) and metates (14 percent) the most common implements (Table 15). When identifiable, the metates were almost always of the trough variety. Additional grinding tools included mortars and pestles, ground slabs, and slabs probably used to sharpen other implements. Polishing stones used in making pottery were also fairly numerous. The most finely made implements were smoothly ground axes with full grooves for hafting.

Although classified as ground stone implements, most of these tools were initially shaped by chipping or pecking with a hammerstone.

TABLE 13.
Distribution of bifacially retouched stone artifacts.

	A.D. 1050–1100					A.D. 1100–1150			Post-A.D. 1050					Undated			
	GC 270	GC 268	GC 329B	GC 378	GC 408	GC 212	GC 212A	GC 215	WP 24	WP 37	WP 72	GC 276	WP 2	WP 5	WP 22	WT Other 10 Sites*	Total
Projectile Points	3			2	3	66	1	16	1	1		1		7		2	103
Unnotched	2			1	1	32		6	1	1		1				1	46
Corner notched				1	1	15	1	5									23
Basally notched														1			1
Side notched	1					1											2
Side & basally notched														1			1
Miscellaneous														2			2
Blanks						15		4						1		1	21
Fragments					1	3		1						2			7
Drills						3		1									4

Type																		Total
Large Thinned Bifaces	1	6	1	1		59	1	7	1		2	5	2	24	2	3	9	124
Unnotched	1	4	1	1		11					2		2	5	1	3	2	33
Corner notched						4								3				7
Side notched						1	1	1	1					2				6
Basally notched						1												1
Backed knives		2				4									1		2	9
Fragments						38		6				5		14			5	68
Unthinned Bifaces		6		3	3	40			1		2		1			2	2	60
Triangular				1		4										1		6
Rectangular		2		1	1	6							1					11
Ovate						6												6
Backed knives		1		1	2	4					1							9
Wide bladed		3				7			1		1						1	13
Cylinders						5										1		6
Fragments						8											1	9
TOTAL	1	12	1	4	3	168	2	30	2	1	4	8	3	32	3	5	12	291

*Includes sites with only 1 artifact: WP3, WP4, WP25, WP29, WP36, WP57, WP65, WP70, WP71, WP77, WT1, and one provenience unknown.

TABLE 14.
Distribution of marginally retouched stone artifacts and core tools.

	Gouge	Scraper	Knife	Scraper/ Knife	Scraper/ Gouge	Knife/ Gouge	Scraper/ Knife/ Gouge	Total Marginally Retouched	Chopper	Hammer- stone
Pre-A.D. 1050?										
GC270	2		3			1	1	7		1
A.D. 1050–1100										
GC268	2	3	3	2	1	2	1	14		
GC329B		1	1					2		1
GC378	3	4	3		3			13	No data	No data
GC408		4	2	1	1			8	No data	No data
GC414A	1	1						2		
A.D. 1100–1150										
GC212	78	119	60	54	67	61	32	471	11	11
GC212A		1	2	2				5		
GC215	42	56	82	51	18	39	10	298	No data	No data
GC265		1						1		

Post-A.D. 1050										
WP14	2							3		
WP24	1	1			2			5	1	
WP37		1		1				2		
WP72		1		1				1		
Undated Sites										
GC276	1	3	2	1		2		10		
WP5	8	18	11	10	4	7		58		
WP6		1	2					3	1	
WP18						1		1		
WP22	1	10		2	1	8	3	25		
WP36	1							1		
WP40				1				1		
WP47						1	1	1		
WP53				1				1		
WP71		1			1	1		2		
WP73						1		1		
WT1			1			1		2		
WT2			1					1		
WT10			1			1		2		
KP1					1	1		2		
TOTAL	142	227	174	127	99	126	48	943	12	13

TABLE 15.
Distribution of ground stone and miscellaneous stone artifacts.

	A.D. 1050–1100						A.D. 1100–1150								
	GC 270	GC 268	GC 329B	GC 378	GC 408	GC 414A	GC 212	GC 212A	GC 215	GC 265	WP 14	WP 37	WP 72	KP 1	TOTAL
GROUND STONE	9	3	2	9	28	9	95	198	123	5	2	1	5	2	491
Metates	3	1		1	1	3	21	5	10					1	46
Trough, open one end	1			1			3	3							8
Trough, open both ends							2								2
Utah type	1														1
Trough, unclassified	1	1			1	1	7	1	7					1	20
Slab									1						1
Unclassified						2	9	1	2						14
Manos	6	2	2	5	20	5	36	15	48	5	2		3	1	150
One surface, rectangular	4	1			6	1	11	5	9				1		38
Two opposed surfaces				3	8	1	9	5	22	2	1				51
Two surfaces on one face	1		1				7	4	2				2	1	20
Three surfaces	1			1	1		8	1	9						21
One surface, triangular									2	1					5
Unclassified		1	1	1	5	2	1		4	2	1				15
Ground Slabs									2						2
Mortars					1		3	1							5

114

Pestles	2				2				2
Sharpening Stones	2	1				1			
Atypical Grinding Stones	3			3					
Axes	12			5	3	2		1	
Pot Lids	5			3		2			
Polishing Stones	17		1	2	2	9		1	2
Square Stones	2					2			
Cylindrical Stones	7			2		4		1	
Stone Balls	1				1				
Flat Discs and Squares	16			2	2	11	1		
Shaped Slabs	8			8					

TABLE 15 (continued).

	A.D. 1050–1100						A.D. 1100–1150								
	GC 270	GC 268	GC 329B	GC 378	GC 408	GC 414A	GC 212	GC 212A	GC 215	GC 265	WP 14	WP 37	WP 72	KP 1	TOTAL
Ornaments															
Beads								143*					1		144
Pendants							2	23*							25
Other ornaments							2	1							3
Unidentifiable Ground Stone Fragments						3			38						41
MISCELLANEOUS STONE	1						9	1							11
Concretion Fetishes	1						2								3
Hematite							4								4
Yellow Ochre							1								1
Turquoise							2								2
Unclassified								1							1
TOTAL GROUND AND MISCELLANEOUS	10	3	2	9	28	9	104	199	123	5	2	1	5	2	502

*All from one bracelet.

116

Once the desired overall shape was achieved, the tools or ornaments were finished by grinding, either as a deliberate part of the manufacturing process or through use. Manos and metates in particular tended to acquire their characteristic forms as they were used. Many manos undoubtedly began in one form but by the time of discard had been worn into a different shape. Thus the "types" of manos described in Appendix D probably represent a series of wear stages more than different intentionally manufactured forms. When the surfaces of grinding tools had been worn too smooth for effective use, they frequently were roughened by pecking with a hammerstone.

Virtually all of the grinding implements found were made of sandstone or limestone from the Kaibab formation, both of which are soft, granular, abrasive materials well suited to this purpose. The sandstone ranged from very fine grained to a coarse conglomerate, while the limestone was relatively fine in texture but had a high sand content. For other implements, harder materials were selected. Axes, for example, were manufactured from igneous rock, and pebbles of quartzite or igneous rock were used for polishing ceramic vessels. Vesicular basalt appeared only in a group of small cylindrical objects of unknown function. The softest material employed was mudstone, from which were made small, perforated discs that might have served as spindle whorls. A low-grade turquoise was found in the form of beads and pendants, and several unworked pieces of hematite and yellow ochre probably were intended to be ground for paint pigments.

PRE-PUEBLO STONE ARTIFACTS

Certain projectile points found in the Walhalla Glades (Fig. 34) were identical in form to known western Basketmaker II types dating between about 100 B.C. and A.D. 500 (Reinhart 1969:92). They included three large side-notched points and one large corner-notched point from site WP5, a heavy concentration of stone artifacts probably representing a hunting camp near Greenland Lake. A second large corner-notched point was found as an isolated artifact in the same area, and another side-notched point of the Basketmaker type was picked up at an unrecorded location. Finally, a large side-notched fragment from site GC212 probably was a Basketmaker point that had been found and taken home by a later Pueblo inhabitant of the Walhalla Glades.

FIG. 34. Probable Basketmaker projectile points.

The entire lithic collection from site WP5 differed in one major respect from the lithic assemblages of Pueblo sites in the Walhalla Glades: it included no ground stone artifacts. Its chipped stone material was not entirely different from that of the Pueblo sites, consisting of large quantities of debitage and utilized flakes and smaller numbers of retouched tools. However, there was a greater proportion of exotic chert in all the categories of chipped stone artifacts at WP5 than elsewhere, and large projectile points outnumbered small ones. There were no small unnotched or corner-notched points, whereas these were two of the more common types at Pueblo sites.

It is obvious that some Pueblos used the area around Greenland

Lake, for ceramics dating between A.D. 1050 and 1150 were also found at WP5. Much of the lithic material from the site probably represents this Pueblo period, and the differences between this assemblage and those of the habitation sites are probably due to the specialized hunting of large game, presumably mule deer, that took place at Greenland Lake. However, the presence of seven probable Basketmaker projectile points indicates that people camped and hunted at the sinkhole long before the Pueblo farmers of the eleventh century arrived on the Walhalla Plateau.

6
Summary and Discussion

Having described all the disparate aspects of the archaeological remains of the Walhalla Glades—site distribution, architecture, ceramics, stone artifacts, and so forth—we can summarize our findings and add some further interpretations to those already ventured. First, a basic question must be addressed: What conditions made the plateau suitable for agriculture in the past? Second, our opinions about the answer to this question will be integrated with a summary of the prehistory of the Walhalla Glades. And finally, an attempt will be made to relate events on the plateau to contemporaneous developments in the Grand Canyon.

THE PROBLEM OF AGRICULTURE

Efforts to grow experimental gardens in the Walhalla Glades in 1969 and 1970 met with one serious problem, a lack of rain for about three weeks immediately after planting, when moisture was essential for seed germination. This spring drought, combined with the present scarcity of water sources in the Glades, suggests that some climatic difference must have existed prehistorically to make dry farming more feasible then than it is today. The locations of sites on relatively flat areas not suited for extensive catchment of runoff seems further evidence that rainfall was sufficient for dry farming during the prehistoric occupation.

Among the alternative kinds of climatic change that might account for the prehistoric situation, the most direct would simply be a slight shift in the yearly distribution of precipitation that eliminated the spring drought or at least caused the summer rains to begin by mid-June instead of July. Without the need for hand watering to ensure germination, farming probably would have been possible in all years except those of severe drought. Unfortunately, we have no evidence either for or against such a subtle shift in rainfall patterns, and this line of thinking can only be speculative.

Another possibility is that precipitation was once greater than it is at present, regardless of its distribution. An annual increase might have meant heavier spring rainfall, or it might have brought more winter snow that remained as soil moisture longer into the spring. Evidence of increased precipitation during portions of the 100-year occupation of the Walhalla Glades comes from tree-ring data published by Dean and Robinson (1977). Originally presented as a series of maps illustrating relative variability in precipitation and temperature in the Southwest between A.D. 680 and 1969, these data were used to plot the graph shown in Figure 35. Each numerical value on the graph represents the departure, measured in standard deviations, of annual tree growth in a ten-year interval from an index of mean growth for the entire tree-ring chronology. Because none of the tree-ring sources used in constructing the original maps were in the Grand Canyon, our graph uses the interpolated values for isopleths shown on the maps as running through or very near the canyon. Presumably these data give a more accurate picture of precipitation variability in our immediate study area. Because tree growth mainly reflects annual precipitation and temperature, positive departures on the graph indicate greater-than-normal rainfall and lower-than-normal temperatures, negative departures the opposite (Dean and Robinson 1977:8).

Figure 35 shows three intervals between A.D. 1050 and 1150 when tree growth, and thus presumably annual precipitation, was more than one standard deviation above the mean in the Grand Canyon region. The use of the Walhalla Glades could have centered around wet periods between A.D. 1040 and 1070, A.D. 1080 and 1090, and A.D. 1110 and 1120. However, there is a problem in assuming such a correlation because as was previously noted, higher annual precipitation tends to be accompanied by lower temperatures. The growing season of the Glades has been barely adequate in recent years when precipitation

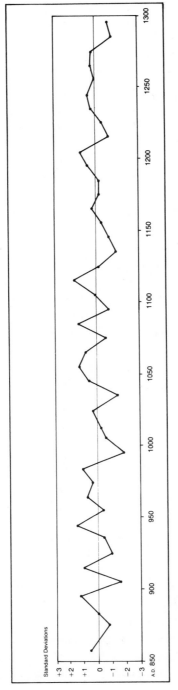

FIG. 35. Dendroclimatic curve for the Grand Canyon, based on data from Dean and Robinson (1977).

was below average. Any further decrease in average annual temperature, accompanying an increase in precipitation, might have reduced the frost-free period to a length insufficient for crop maturation.

We know that Pueblo farmers did raise crops successfully in the Walhalla Glades, and we believe that they were more likely to have done so during periods of increased, rather than decreased, precipitation. The question is, then, do the Walhalla Glades offer any special environmental conditions that would have mitigated the postulated lowering of temperatures when rainfall increased? Perhaps the answer lies in the unique geographic situation of the Glades, which are surrounded on three sides by the Grand Canyon and thus receive warm updrafts that may help to moderate the climate. Not only are the Walhalla Glades situated in this manner but so is the entire Walhalla Plateau of which the Glades are a sort of appendage. Immediately north of the Glades is a higher land area on the Walhalla Plateau that in turn gives way again to canyon terrain. It seems likely that warm air rising from the canyon north of the Walhalla Plateau cools over the higher land mass and flows downward from north to south along the drainage valleys that dissect the Glades. The higher ridges, south-exposed and warmed by updrafts from the surrounding canyon, might get slightly warmer temperatures than would be predicted on the basis of the elevation of the plateau. Planting in these favorable locations, the Pueblo farmers might have been able to raise crops to maturity before the first fall frost.

Obviously, without a thorough meteorological study of the Walhalla Plateau, the preceding explanation remains largely conjectural. Yet we are forced to the conclusion that some special environmental attribute of the Walhalla Glades made them more attractive to Pueblo farmers than we would have anticipated. Lacking better evidence, we assume that increased rainfall and a favorable geographic and topographic situation allowed successful farming in the Walhalla Glades at times between A.D. 1050 and 1150.

THE PREHISTORY OF THE WALHALLA GLADES

The earliest known use of the Walhalla Plateau was by small hunting parties during the Basketmaker II period of about 100 B.C. to A.D. 500, and this use probably had little to do with climate. The sinkhole now known as Greenland Lake, an ideal watering place for mule deer, must have attracted Archaic hunters as it did the later Pueblos. While the Walhalla Plateau, presumably including the Walhalla Glades, was part of the hunting territory of these Basketmaker people, it does not seem to have served them as a permanent home. Instead, temporary hunting camps seem to be the only kinds of sites for which traces remain in the area.

A.D. 1050–1100

Exactly when Pueblo agriculturalists began moving onto the plateau is uncertain, but the time was apparently between A.D. 950 and 1050. By 1050, the Walhalla Glades must have become eminently suitable for farming, thanks to a period of above-average rainfall that began about A.D. 1040. In response, small field houses associated with artificial terraces, garden plots, and check dams began to appear in every area in the Glades.

The locations selected for cultivation offered a combination of advantages. Situated on the upper slopes or the relatively flat tops of ridges, the fields may have been warmed by air rising from the canyon, and they avoided, we suspect, the cooler temperatures resulting from cold air drainage through the intervening valleys. The hazards of erosion would also have been minimized by such locations or at least would have been kept to proportions manageable through terracing. Behind the terraces, soil moisture was retained longer, and the soil itself was replenished by the capture of waterborne silt. Where possible, small tributary arroyos were dammed, presumably to divert runoff into adjacent gardens. However, check dams do not seem to have been extensively used, either because of the steepness of the drainages or because increased rainfall made them unnecessary. Pollen samples, including several taken from the soil behind terraces, indicate that all three of the southwestern staples—corn, beans, and squash—were grown.

Adjacent to their fields, the Pueblo farmers built small masonry structures from the plentiful Kaibab limestone of the plateau. These structures usually comprised only one or two rooms, occasionally three or four. They were remarkably devoid of features, usually consisting simply of four walls, a beam-and-pole roof, and a floor of hard-packed

125

earth. Because of the scarcity of hearths and other features and because so little artifactual material was found upon excavation, it seems likely that these rooms were never inhabited by many people or for long periods of time. Most of the rooms were quite small, averaging about 7 square meters in floor space, and were probably used mainly for storage of the harvested crops. However, some food processing such as the grinding of corn was indicated by manos, metates, and other implements recovered from the sites. Presumably at least some of the structures were also used for shelter by farmers temporarily resident to tend the fields.

Even assuming a minimum of domestic activities at sites dating between A.D. 1050 and 1100, it was still surprising to find so few features and artifacts obviously associated with cooking, in particular hearths. It might be that such features were located outside rooms at distances great enough that we did not find them when clearing the ground surface around the structures. Or perhaps only some of the sites actually served as domiciles, the others being used for storage and processing by people who lived in habitation rooms elsewhere. Site GC408, a two-room structure of this time period, is a likely example of such a habitation since it produced a relatively large artifact collection and also contained a hearth.

If it is true that not all structures housed people, then the magnitude of occupation during this period would be overestimated by using site counts as indexes of population size. The difficulty of estimating population would be compounded if the locations of fields changed from year to year because of exhaustion of the soil or efforts to prevent that problem. While the terraced areas on hillsides might have received enough new soil each year through slope wash to prevent the loss of all nutrients, the shallow soil of unterraced areas might not have been good for more than a few years of cultivation. Perhaps as new fields were cultivated and old ones abandoned, the structures associated with the disused fields were abandoned too. These rooms may have been dismantled and the building stones and beams reused in new structures, a practice that would account for the lack of wall remains at sites such as GC268, GC329B, and GC414A. Again, if this was the case, the total number of sites in the Walhalla Glades between A.D. 1050 and 1100 would be misleading if used to estimate the size of the population in any one year. Even so, fairly intensive use of the area is unquestionable.

126

Of subsistence activities other than agriculture, we found little direct evidence in the Walhalla Glades. The small amount of animal bone recovered from a few of the sites indicated that at least some hunting took place, and it certainly seems unlikely that the faunal resources of the plateau went unexploited. Small mammals could have been obtained in the vicinity of the sites themselves, and hunting expeditions into the higher elevations around Greenland Lake followed the movement of the deer herd into the fir-spruce forest during the summers. To what extent the wild plant resources of the plateau were used is unknown, but it is doubtful that any plant food other than piñon nuts, in years of a good crop, was abundant enough to have provided a major part of the food supply.

A.D. 1100–1150

Sometime around A.D. 1100, the number of sites in the Walhalla Glades declined significantly. Possibly this decline was related to a dry period between A.D. 1090 and 1100 (Fig. 35), but such a correlation does not explain why the site count failed to return to its previous level when rainfall again increased to a peak between A.D. 1110 and 1120. Presumably the sites dating between A.D. 1100 and 1150 do reflect the favorable agricultural conditions of this wet interval, but the changes in adaptation that apparently took place after A.D. 1100 are not easily interpreted.

To some extent, life continued as before. Most sites were again small structures of limestone masonry located on the ridgetops and upper slopes bordering drainage valleys. Some of the dated sites were associated with agricultural terraces, and there is no reason to believe that farming methods differed from those of the preceding period. However, one-room sites were seldom built, and two-room or three-room sites became the norm. This selective disappearance of a particular type of site probably cannot be explained by a simple decrease in population size, which is itself far from certain. One possible interpretation is that agriculture became more concentrated in a few locations after A.D. 1100, so scattered storage rooms in addition to the storage rooms of the larger sites were no longer necessary. Yet even if this was the case, we still have no good explanation for the concentration of farming itself.

Another puzzling issue is the appearance of the two large sites on the

127

southeastern edge of the Walhalla Glades, GC212/212A and GC215. Actually, site GC212/212A may have had fewer rooms than would seem apparent at first glance, if its two component roomblocks were not in use simultaneously. This may well have been the case, for roomblock GC212 had at some time burned and fallen into ruin, and its rubble was later cleared into what appear to be garden plots on the relatively fertile midden. Most likely the people who used these plots lived in roomblock GC212A, since the two small rooms also erected on the fill of the abandoned site GC212 were unconvincing as habitations.

Even if this site never comprised more than four rooms at a time, the four making up roomblock GC212 were unusually large and contained an unprecedented six hearths. This roomblock also produced much more artifactual material than any other site in the Walhalla Glades, some of which was probably trash but some of which apparently fell into the rooms from the rooftops when the structure burned. Together the hearths and artifacts imply that site GC212/212A saw a longer occupation, more years of reoccupation, a greater population, or all three, than most other sites in the Walhalla Glades.

Perhaps an aggregation of people practicing a full range of domestic activities at one site was made possible by the increased precipitation that favored agriculture between A.D. 1110 and 1120. One year's harvest might have been great enough to support several families throughout the fall, when they could have gathered piñon nuts and hunted deer and bighorn sheep in the canyon, and then throughout the following summer when they returned to the Glades. Conversely, site GC212/212A could represent an attempt later in the settlement sequence to cope with a deteriorating climate by concentrating the labor of more people into agriculture or by increasing the pueblo's storage capacity. Unfortunately, we lack the precise chronological control over sites of the period from A.D. 1100 to 1150 or other evidence that would allow us to choose one interpretation over the other.

As for the 18-room site GC215, its character is not so perplexing as its location on Sky Island, a rock pillar standing away from the plateau. From the small size of most rooms, the presence of one hearth, and the recovery of large numbers of artifacts, it could be inferred that the site functioned as a storage facility, a food processing area, and, to some extent, a habitation. The number of rooms suggests that here, as at GC212, a group of families had joined to prepare and store their crops communally.

But why was the site situated on a pillar requiring such effort to reach? Were the advantages of this location shared by Wotan's Throne, a larger rock "island" where a few crude structures, two cliff granaries, and a possible terrace were built? Perhaps the isolation of these places enhanced the protection of stored food, though we have no indication that a defensible location was ever important in the Walhalla Glades. Possibly these sites were bases for the hunting of deer and bighorn in the canyon, for a relatively large number of artiodactyl bones were recovered from GC215, and several projectile points from Wotan's Throne. Nevertheless, we cannot as yet offer any plausible explanation for the expansion to these unusual locations after A.D. 1100.

The drought that began about A.D. 1130 (Fig. 35) continued virtually unabated for more than a century (Dean and Robinson 1977). The Walhalla Glades, despite their high rainfall relative to that of the Grand Canyon, must have become a precarious place for farming. Consequently, by at least A.D. 1150 and probably a decade or two earlier, the summer inhabitants of the plateau ceased to return.

RELATIONSHIPS BETWEEN PLATEAU AND CANYON

We have already mentioned that archaeological evidence such as scarcity of hearths leads us to believe that the Walhalla Glades were occupied only in the summer and early fall. To this evidence could be added that of the severe winters of the plateau, which offer few incentives for anyone to live there year-round. In spite of certain moderating factors, the Walhalla Glades are still snowbound all or most of the winter, and the deer herd leaves the plateau then for the lower piñon-juniper zone. But if summer residence was indeed the case, where did the farmers live during the rest of the year? To answer this question, we look to the Grand Canyon itself.

Obviously the canyon remains fairly warm all year, with an average annual temperature of more than 15 degrees C (60 degrees F.). In fact, the long growing season on the canyon floor likely permitted an early spring and a late fall crop to be raised that were in addition to the summer harvest produced on the plateau. All the canyon resources—for example, deer, bighorn, agave, and yucca—are as accessible from the canyon floor as from the rim, and other productive plants such as mesquite and prickly-pear are also available at the lower elevations.

For these reasons, it seems highly probable that the farmers who inhabited the Walhalla Glades during the summers were the same ones who spent the rest of the year at the many known sites in the side canyons surrounding the Glades and in river-edge locations such as Unkar and Bright Angel deltas (Schwartz, Marshall, and Kepp 1979; Schwartz, Chapman, and Kepp 1980).

Among the canyon sites excavated by SAR during earlier projects were many that were large in comparison to sites in the Walhalla Glades. At Unkar Delta, for example, the largest unit pueblo had seven contiguous habitation and storage rooms, and single-room sites were the exception. Average room size at Unkar was 8.4 square meters, as compared with the average size of 7.4 square meters for rooms in the Walhalla Glades sites. Most of the excavated sites in the canyon yielded large quantities of artifacts and other cultural debris, suggesting a considerable length of occupation, fairly large populations, or both. In addition, hearths were common at the excavated canyon sites, occurring both inside and outside rooms at nearly every pueblo. All these characteristics suggest that the sites on the canyon floor served as habitations that were fairly continuously occupied. They could easily have been the permanent homes of the farmers who cultivated crops during the summer in the Walhalla Glades.

Seasonal habitation might also help to explain the absence of kivas from the Walhalla Glades. Several depressions thought possibly to represent subterranean kivas were tested but proved to be nothing more than shallow borrow pits. Nor did any of the excavated surface rooms give any indication of having been used for ceremonial purposes. The argument that kivas were lacking because the shallow soil above bedrock prevented their construction was rejected on the grounds that shallow but recognizable kivas had been found at Tusayan Ruin on the South Rim (Haury 1931), where the Kaibab formation offers the same kind of geological substratum as that found in the Walhalla Glades. Because four kivas had been excavated in the Grand Canyon during SAR projects, we wondered at first whether the absence of kivas in the Glades might mean that the people of the plateau and those of the canyon were two distinct cultural groups. However, we now think it more likely that one group of people existed and that they built ceremonial structures only at their winter habitations, where population was concentrated for longer periods of time.

Besides the presence or absence of kivas, there are other differences between sites of the Walhalla Glades and those of the Grand Canyon that might be construed as evidence for two distinct groups of people. For example, some types of pottery varied in quantity from one location to the other, and a few types of stone tools were limited to either plateau or canyon. However, such differences could instead be interpreted functionally, and in general the sites and artifacts of the two locations were similar enough that they could easily have been left by a single population.

Architecturally, the canyon sites resembled those of the plateau in that they consisted of rectangular rooms of limestone or other masonry built in linear units. Descriptions of these sites have been presented elsewhere (Schwartz, Chapman, and Kepp 1980) and will not be repeated here. Suffice it to say that we feel the differences between these sites and those of the plateau stem from winter versus summer use, variability in local building materials, and other such factors. Furthermore, agricultural features found at Unkar Delta in the canyon included artificial terraces, check dams, and garden plots identical to those seen in the Walhalla Glades. One large site on the delta had even been cleared and used for farming after it had fallen into ruin, just as had been done at site GC212 in the Walhalla Glades. From these similarities, we surmise that agricultural methods used on the plateau were repeated in the canyon.

In terms of pottery, sites of the plateau and the canyon were obviously part of a single ceramic tradition because they produced exactly the same wares and types. However, many pottery types were relatively abundant or scarce in the Walhalla Glades compared with those found at Unkar Delta, which is our main source of information for the canyon. Implements used in pottery manufacture were found at sites in both locations, and it might be that frequency differences resulted from the production of different types for functionally different purposes in each location or from variation in available raw materials. Or perhaps certain kinds of pottery were imported by these people when they were living in the canyon and other types when they were in residence on the plateau, depending on the geographic proximity of the trade sources. Lacking better evidence about where each type of pottery was manufactured, we cannot state with certainty that the observed ceramic frequency differences do not represent differences between the people involved, but we think it more likely that another explanation exists.

With the exception of a few implement types, the stone tool industries of the plateau and the canyon were virtually identical. Again, the exceptions can probably be explained functionally. For example, the contrast between the finely made axes of the Walhalla Glades and the crude specimens from Unkar Delta likely reflects the fact that the plateau is heavily forested, while the only timber available on Unkar Delta is driftwood. Both industries emphasized the expedient manufacture of flake tools with little, if any, retouch modification but with each flake used for multiple purposes. The more formalized chipped stone tools and the ground stone implements included the same range of types in each location, differing mainly in the kinds of locally available raw materials that were used. The entire process of chipped stone tool manufacture was represented in both assemblages by tools ranging from cores to finished implements.

We certainly would not go so far as to say that the inhabitants of a particular site in the Walhalla Glades were the same people who occupied another specific site in the canyon. But to say that in general the farmers of the Glades were the same people who lived in the side canyons and riverside sites of the Grand Canyon seems warranted on the basis of strong similarities in both material culture and economic adaptation.

Elsewhere we discussed evidence for the temporary abandonment of canyon sites during periods of below-average precipitation (Schwartz, Chapman, and Kepp 1980). Whether the same kind of exodus occurred on the plateau is not clear, because changes through time in architecture and site distribution were not as marked there as on Unkar Delta, and the pottery samples from North Rim sites were generally too small to permit fine chronological control. It is possible that the plateau too was abandoned during these dry intervals, the inhabitants moving to a location such as the Houserock Valley northeast of the Walhalla Plateau. However, the nature of population movements within the Grand Canyon region remains one of our major uncertainties.

The ultimate abandonment of the Walhalla Glades was undoubtedly connected with that of sites in the Grand Canyon. If the economic adaptation even during times of above-average precipitation involved farming in as many places as possible, then presumably a decline in rainfall that affected either the plateau or the canyon would have jeopardized the entire system. According to the tree-ring data, such a decline did take place between A.D. 1130 and 1150, during which time the population of the Grand Canyon region almost completely disappeared.

Appendix A

SITE DESCRIPTIONS

In this appendix are described all the sites recorded by the School of American Research field crew, including sites originally catalogued by Edward T. Hall (1942) that were definitely relocated and identified by SAR. The sites are grouped in chronological order within the following categories: pre-A.D. 1050, A.D. 1050–1100, A.D. 1100–1150, post-A.D. 1050, and undated sites. In each group, the sites are arranged in numerical order, all those with "GC" prefixes preceding those with "WP" prefixes.

During excavation, features were numbered consecutively in the order in which they were discovered, for example, "room 1," "hearth 2," and "burial 3." Consequently, "room 3" at a site was not necessarily the third room found but only the third feature assigned a number. Thus the room numbers mentioned in the descriptions should be considered simply as nominal designations and not as quantitative measures.

The site plans accompanying the descriptions of the excavated sites provide some information that, because of length limitations, has been omitted from the text. This information includes some dimensions not specifically mentioned in the text, the orientation of rooms and other features, and the spatial relationships of features to one another. When dimensions are given in the text, they are always interior measurements. For simplicity, only the four cardinal directions are used in describing the walls of rooms; for example, the "north" wall of a room may not have lain due north from the center of the room but was closest to that direction.

POSSIBLE PRE-A.D. 1050 SITE

GC270

Site GC270 (Fig. 36) consisted of a single masonry room situated near the northern edge of a wide ridge in open ponderosa pine forest. The room was completely excavated and appeared to represent one occupation, probably a brief one. Large areas outside the room were stripped, but no additional architectural features were found.

The rectangular room measured approximately 3.1 m by 3.3 m, with its remaining walls standing no more than two courses or about 30 cm high. All four walls were built directly on the original ground surface. The north and south walls consisted of two courses each of horizontally placed, shaped limestone blocks. The east wall was a single course of vertically set blocks, and the west wall included a foundation course of cobbles and an upper course of horizontally placed slabs and blocks. The wall elements were aligned to form an even face on the exterior of the room. Fallen portions of the walls would have brought the original walls to an estimated height of at least 96 cm.

The floor consisted of a 2-cm-thick layer of sandy clay with inclusions of pebbles, laid directly on the original ground surface. A possible fire pit was found near the center of the room. It was nearly circular, basin shaped and unlined, measuring 58–64 cm in diameter and 28 cm deep. A little ash and burned clay were found in the pit fill. In a few places, the sides of the pit had been fired, though not to the same extent as other fire pits found on the Walhalla Plateau. No evidence of a roof was seen.

The fill of this structure was a fine soil containing small pebbles and lumps of clay but little cultural material.

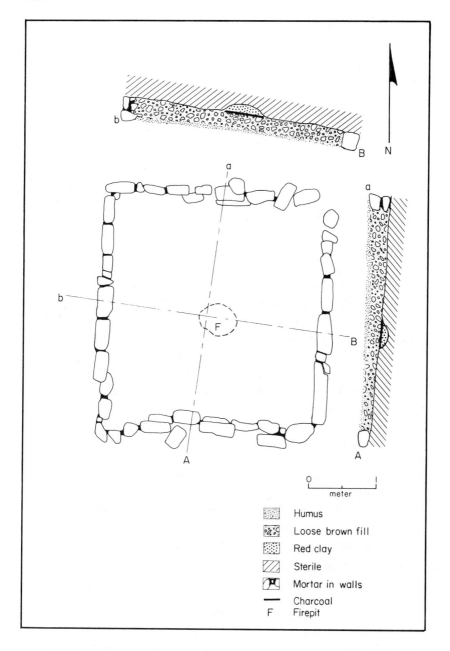

FIG. 36. Plan of site GC270.

SITES DATING BETWEEN A.D. 1050 AND 1100

GC268

Site GC268, located on a ridge in ponderosa pine forest, included at least one and probably two contiguous masonry rooms and a series of four agricultural terraces that lay directly east of the roomblock (Figs. 37 and 38). One room was completely excavated and the terraces were tested by trenching. A single occupation of the site was indicated.

The excavated room measured approximately 2.1 m by 2.6 m, its walls standing no higher than three courses or 32 cm high. All four walls were constructed of horizontally placed limestone slabs that were fairly evenly aligned, especially on the interior of the room. The foundation courses had been laid in shallow trenches. Some slabs in the upper courses had been shaped by pecking. Fallen wall elements would have brought the original walls to an estimated height of about 70 cm.

The hard, clearly defined floor consisted of a layer of adobe 2–3 cm thick, laid directly on the ground surface. Three depressions or possible cists were found in the floor; all were unlined, oval to circular, and filled with roof fall. They measured 82–93 cm in diameter and 9 cm deep, 52–76 cm in diameter and 6 cm deep, and 18 cm in diameter and 9 cm deep, respectively.

A layer of hard-packed adobe 12–14 cm thick and lying directly on the floor may have been the remains of the roof. However, no beams, beam impressions, or chunks of adobe were found. Above this layer were 15 cm of loose fill containing some cultural material.

Four parallel terrace alignments lay about 5 meters east of the excavated room. These were constructed of drylaid cobbles stacked 15–20 cm high from the original ground surface. They averaged 14 m in length, were situated about 75 cm apart, and held back accumulations of fill about 15 cm deep.

GC309

Site GC309 was an L-shaped roomblock with one large room as its east-west arm and at least two smaller rooms as the north-south arm. It lay near the top of a west-facing slope in open ponderosa-piñon forest

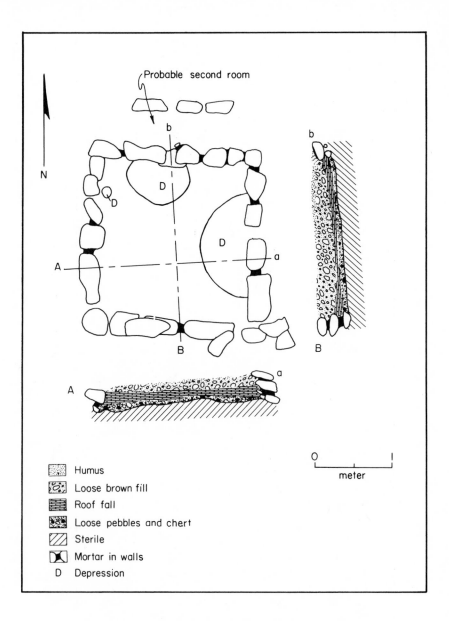

Humus
Loose brown fill
Roof fall
Loose pebbles and chert
Sterile
Mortar in walls
D   Depression

FIG. 37. Plan of excavated room at site GC268.

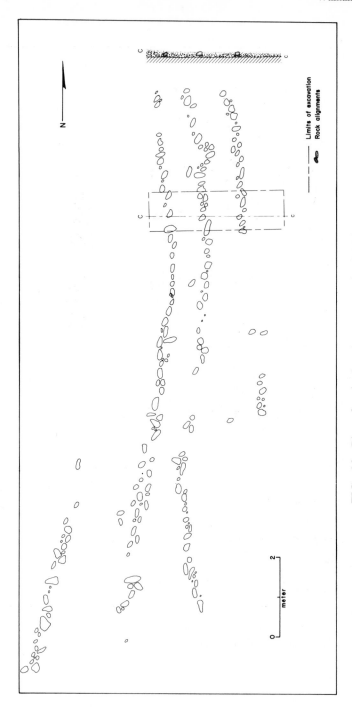

FIG. 38. Plan of agricultural terraces at site GC268.

close to the rim of the Grand Canyon. One of the small rooms (1.7 m by 2.2 m) was excavated (Fig. 39).

The north, east, and west walls of the excavated room were constructed of limestone blocks and slabs laid horizontally on the original ground surface. The slabs had been shaped by pecking and were evenly aligned on the room interior, with small pebbles used as chinking. The south wall was of drylaid, unshaped blocks that were not evenly aligned. None of the walls stood more than two courses or 35 cm high, but fallen elements would have brought the height to an estimated 1.4 m.

The original ground surface had apparently been used without alteration as the floor of the excavated room. A layer of fill including chunks of adobe lay directly on the floor and possibly was evidence of a roof. This layer was overlain by some 20 cm of loose soil, and neither layer yielded much cultural material.

GC329B

Site GC329B consisted of two contiguous masonry rooms located near the north edge of a ridge in open ponderosa pine forest. The northernmost room, measuring approximately 2.8 m by 3.3 m, was considerably larger than the adjacent room. The larger room was completely excavated (Fig. 40).

All four walls were constructed of limestone blocks and slabs that had been shaped by chipping and laid horizontally on the original ground surface. The elements in the north and west walls were more evenly aligned on the room interior, those in the east and south walls more so on the exterior. Mortar and small chinking stones had been used generously to finish the unevenly aligned wall faces and to maintain level coursing. The remaining walls stood at a maximum height of 35 cm, but fallen elements would have brought the walls to an estimated 70 cm.

The floor of the excavated room was a 4-cm-thick layer of sandy soil containing small pebbles covering the original ground surface. A charred fragment of a post 5 cm in diameter was set 5 cm into the floor in the southeast corner. Four pieces of sandstone had been used as wedges to stabilize the post. A similar charred post fragment was found in the southwest corner, its butt resting on the floor. A few fragments of charred beams 4 cm in diameter lay on the floor and may have been the remains of the roof.

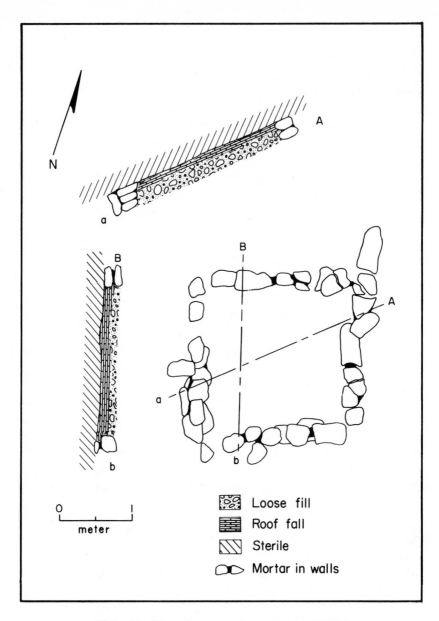

FIG. 39. Plan of excavated room at site GC309.

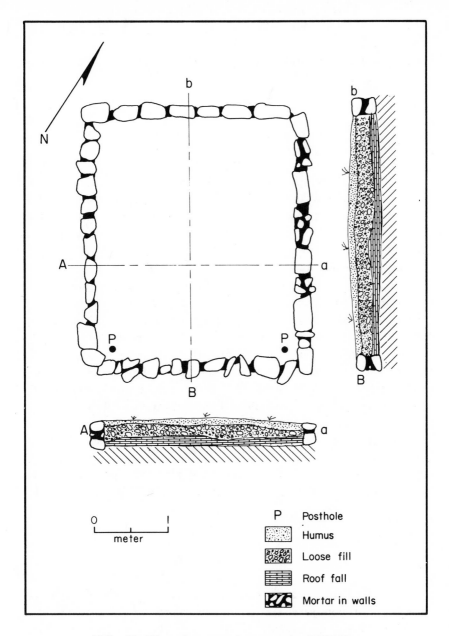

FIG. 40. Plan of excavated room at site GC329B.

The fill of the room consisted of 18 cm of black humus overlying a layer identified as roof fall, which contained the charred beam fragments. Both the "roof fall" layer and the floor yielded a relatively large amount of cultural material, including two manos and a broken Shinarump Corrugated vessel.

GC378

Site GC378 (see Fig. 11) was a shallow masonry room located in open ponderosa grassland on the western edge of the Walhalla Glades, about 9 m from the rim of Clear Creek Canyon. There were no other obvious architectural features at the site, and surface stripping outside the room revealed only a use surface 10–15 cm below the present ground level.

Only the foundations of the north and west walls of the room were standing, each 2.8 m long, but wall fall to the east and south indicated that walls had once been present on all sides. Apparently the east and south walls had been destroyed by heavy root infiltration from nearby trees. The north wall was of unshaped limestone blocks and slabs evenly aligned on the interior and laid horizontally on the original ground surface. The west wall was composed of similar slabs placed vertically and less evenly aligned. There was no good indication of mortar in either wall. Remaining wall height was 15–37 cm, but fallen elements would have brought the height to an estimated 1.5 m.

The room's floor was a natural layer of clay that had been leveled for use. No evidence of a roof was seen. The fill consisted of compact, clayey soil about 15 cm deep, overlain by pine duff. Neither the room nor the outside areas that were stripped produced a great deal of cultural material.

GC408

Site GC408 was situated on an east-sloping ridge in open ponderosa pine forest. It comprised two contiguous rooms and an outlying wall, all of which were excavated (Fig. 41). Room 1, the first structure built at the site, measured 1.8 m by 3.0 m; the adjacent room to the north, room 2, was 3.0 m by 3.6 m. No other architectural features were visible on the site surface or found during stripping outside the rooms.

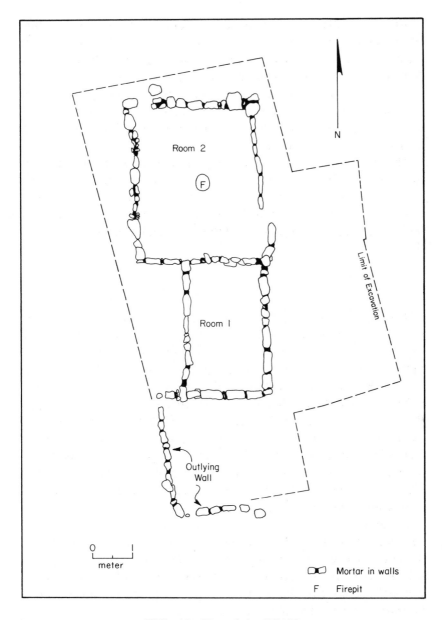

FIG. 41. Plan of site GC408.

Room 1

All four walls were constructed of horizontally placed limestone blocks and slabs, many of which had been pecked to shape. The elements were quite evenly aligned on the exterior of the room. The foundation courses of the north and south walls rested on a layer of adobe mortar, while those of the east and west walls lay directly on the original ground surface. Remaining wall height was a maximum of 52 cm (three courses), and fallen elements would have brought the walls to an estimated height of 1 m.

The original ground surface had apparently been used without alteration as the room floor. A layer of adobe 10–15 cm thick lying above the floor might have been the remains of a roof, but no good evidence of roof fall was found. Except for the fragments of a pottery vessel that lay on the floor, room 1 produced little artifactual material.

Room 2

The walls of this room probably consisted of low masonry foundations with jacal (beam and adobe) superstructures. None of the remaining walls stood more than 38 cm high, and little rock wall fall was seen in the fill. Concentrations of burned, beam-impressed adobe along the north, east, and west walls suggested the presence of jacal upper walls.

The south wall foundation was constructed by extending the previously existing north wall of room 1 about 1.2 m to the west. The extension was composed of two large limestone slabs laid horizontally on the original ground surface. The foundation courses of the north and west walls were built in the same manner, but pebbles and cobbles were used extensively for chinking. The east wall foundation was built of smaller, vertically laid slabs.

In the east wall at the southeast corner was a possible ground-level entrance 42 cm wide. No wall elements were present there, but no definite evidence for an entrance was observed. Another gap was present in the north wall at the northwest corner. Except for a fairly well-defined layer of clay 5 cm thick that lay near the southern end of the room, no definable floor was found in room 2.

A circular fire pit 39 cm in diameter and 22 cm deep lay in the center of the room. Its bottom was lined with cobbles, and it contained ash and roof fall. No actual postholes were found, but two cases of burned beam fragments in the corners of the room pointed to the possibility that corner posts had rested on the floor.

A layer of fill directly above the floor contained burned adobe, some pieces with beam or pole impressions, and charcoal. It was impossible to distinguish roof fall from jacal wall fall, but both may have been represented. A large amount of cultural material, including several manos and pottery vessels, occurred in this level. The overlying layer of sandy soil produced little artifactual material.

Outlying Wall

An L-shaped wall of limestone slabs extended 2.8 m south from the west wall of room 1. It postdated the construction of room 1, although the slabs were laid on the original ground surface. No definite floor was associated with the wall, and it did not appear to be part of a roofed structure.

GC414A

Site GC414A was situated on a ridge sloping gently to the south in open ponderosa pine forest. The site comprised a single masonry room that was completely excavated (Fig. 42). No other architectural features were visible from the surface.

The excavated room measured approximately 2.2 m by 3.1 m, and remaining wall height was no more than two courses or 40 cm. All four walls were constructed of horizontally placed limestone slabs, a few of which had been shaped by pecking. The foundation courses were set on a layer of adobe mortar, and considerable amounts of mortar were used in the walls. The south and west walls were evenly aligned on the room interior and had two well-defined courses. The north and east walls were not evenly faced and contained no definable courses. Fallen wall elements in the fill would have brought the walls to an estimated height of 1 m.

The original ground surface was apparently used without alteration as the room floor. A circular, unlined subfloor cist was found in the southwest corner; it measured 90 cm in diameter and 15 cm deep and

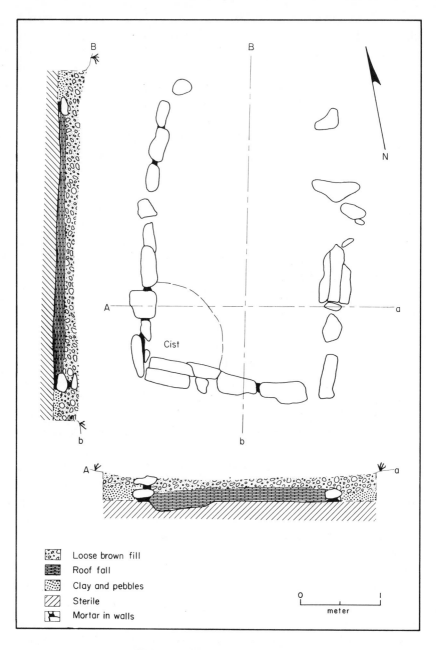

FIG. 42. Plan of site GC414A.

was filled with roof fall. The roof fall was a layer of burned adobe chunks and pieces of charcoal lying directly on the floor. A fairly large amount of cultural material, including several manos and large portions of three pots, was found in the roof-fall layer. Additional material was recovered in four test trenches dug outside the room, adjacent to the walls.

SITES DATING BETWEEN A.D. 1100 AND 1150

GC212/212A

Site GC212/212A (Fig. 43) was located on a ridgetop in open ponderosa pine forest about 150 m from the rim of the Grand Canyon and 50 m west of the Cape Royal road. The portion of the site designated as GC212 consisted of a linear roomblock of four large rooms and, almost adjacent on the west, two small, noncontiguous rooms oriented parallel to the main block. All of these rooms were completely excavated. It appeared that the southernmost rooms of the main block, rooms 11 and 12, were together the first structures built. However, their walls lay over at least three earlier borrow pits whose fill contained sherds and charcoal, suggesting that some occupation of the site occurred prior to the construction of these rooms.

Later, the two larger rooms, 22 and 34, were added to the north of rooms 11 and 12. It is uncertain whether the earlier rooms continued to be occupied at this time, but no evidence to the contrary was found. At a still later date, the small rooms 9 and 44 were built on a layer of fill that had accumulated outside the main roomblock. Again, these features may or may not have been used simultaneously with the larger rooms.

Next in the sequence of events at GC212, the four large rooms, and perhaps the two small ones as well, were abandoned, the roofs of the large rooms apparently having burned. The rooms produced such large quantities of sherds and lithics in their roof fall layers that it seems likely they were used as trash dumps for a time. After some deterioration of the walls had occurred, the fallen rubble was cleared to form a series of roughly rectangular plots or enclosures. It is possible, though far from certain, that these late enclosures were associated with the

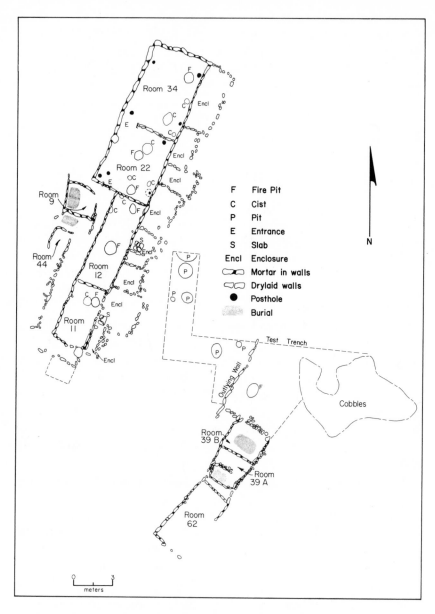

FIG. 43. Plan of site GC212/212A.

148

small rooms 9 and 44, for they lay only slightly higher in the fill than did the walls of the rooms.

In the fill of room 9 and in the area between rooms 9 and 44 were found two burials, an old adult male and a younger one, whose interments were probably the last events at GC212. Along with the two adult females recovered from GC212A, these burials were unique on the Walhalla Plateau. The skeletons and their accompanying grave goods are described in detail in Appendix B.

The portion of the site designated as GC212A lay 11 m east of the GC212 roomblock. It included three contiguous rooms in a linear block, an outlying wall and fire pit, and a paved surface outside the roomblock. All of two rooms and half of the third were excavated, and the outlying areas were tested. No sequence of construction or abandonment could be recognized, although the placement of the two burials appeared to have been the final activity in the roomblock.

GC212

Rooms 11 and 12. These rooms were built as a single unit with a dividing wall between them. They measured approximately 2.3 m by 4.4 m and 2.3 m by 6.8 m, respectively. All the walls were of shaped limestone slabs laid directly on the original ground surface and mortared in horizontal position. The slabs in the four corners of the unit interlocked in alternating courses, whereas the dividing wall between the rooms abutted the east and west walls and did not interlock. The slabs were generally dressed and evenly aligned on the exterior of the rooms. Remaining wall height was 17–50 cm, but the large quantity of wall fall inside and outside the rooms suggested that the walls were originally of masonry to their full height.

No indications of entrances were found in the walls themselves, but just outside and to the east of each room was found a shaped schist slab that lay on an accumulation of fill. These slabs probably were the fallen covers for above-ground wall entrances. They measured 68 cm by 51 cm and 66 cm by 56 cm, respectively.

In both rooms, the original clay ground surface was apparently used without alteration as the floor. Room 11 contained a circular, unlined, basin-shaped fire pit located against the east wall. It measured 75 cm in diameter and 20 cm deep and was filled with ash and small pieces of charcoal. In the center of room 12 was a circular, unlined fire pit with a cross section in the form of an inverted bell. Its dimensions were 96 cm top diameter, 40 cm bottom diameter, and 24 cm deep. A second fire pit near the north wall of room 12 was an oval, basin-shaped pit partially lined with sandstone slabs and measuring 51–65 cm in diameter and 16 cm deep. Both the fire pits in room 12 were filled with ash and charcoal.

Room 11 contained a circular, unlined, basin-shaped cist 62 cm in diameter, 11 cm deep, and filled with sterile clay. Beneath the east wall of room 11 and the north and west walls of room 12 were three unlined, circular cists or borrow pits, all filled with clay and a few sherds and bits of charcoal. They measured 74 cm, 35 cm, and 57 cm in diameter, respectively, and were all 11–12 cm deep.

Roof fall consisted of a layer of burned and unburned adobe chunks lying directly on the floor in each room. This layer contained charcoal and large amounts of cultural material, and in room 12 were found pieces of beam-impressed adobe and a few fragments of charred beams.

Rooms 22 and 34. Both of these very large rooms were added as a single unit to the north wall of room 12, which was lengthened on the west with a 1.75-meter section of vertically placed slabs. All the other walls in the unit were built of large, unshaped limestone blocks set vertically or horizontally on edge. The east wall lay on 5–10 cm of fill, but the others were directly on the original ground surface. The interiors and exteriors of the walls were equally well faced, occasionally with thin, vertically placed slabs on the interior. Remaining wall height was 9–91 cm, except for one particularly large slab that stood 1.24 cm high in the north wall of room 34. From the amount of wall fall in the fill, including a nine-course section visible to the east of room 34, it is assumed that the walls were of masonry up to the roof.

The dividing wall that separated rooms 22 and 34 did not extend entirely across the unit but ended 1.35 m short of the west wall, indicating that the two were joined by an entrance. In addition, a possible sealed, floor-level entrance was noted in the south wall of room 22, where a space between two large slabs was filled with small, drylaid cobbles. In room 34, pieces of a schist slab originally measuring 64 cm by 27 cm were found scattered in the roof fall and may have been a cover for a roof entrance.

In both rooms, the original clay ground surface was apparently used

150

unaltered as the floor. In the floor of room 22 were two fire pits, one near the center of the room and one near the south wall. The former was an unlined, circular, basin-shaped pit measuring 64–72 cm in diameter and 14 cm deep and filled with ash. The second pit was circular with straight sides and lined on the bottom with small limestone cobbles. It was filled with ash and roof fall and measured 63–71 cm in diameter and 23 cm deep. Room 34 contained an unlined, circular, basin-shaped fire pit in the northeast corner. Its dimensions were 79 cm in diameter and 24 cm deep, and it was filled with ash, charcoal, and pieces of burned adobe.

Each room also contained three subfloor cists, all unlined and circular to oblong in outline. They ranged from 26 cm to 90 cm in diameter and from 4 cm to 26 cm deep. One cist in room 22 was filled with culturally sterile clay and another with roof fall; all the others contained clay and trash. A large cist or borrow pit, 96–136 cm in diameter and 18–58 cm deep, lay beneath the west wall of room 22.

Four postholes were found in room 22. In the northeast corner was a hole 38 cm in diameter and 28 cm deep, partially lined with limestone cobbles so that it would have held a post about 15 cm in diameter. In the southeast corner a post had been set in a deep hole (63 cm) dug through a previously existing, shallow pit. This posthole measured 16 cm in diameter, and the charred remains of a post were found above it. Two postholes were located in the southwest corner of room 22, one of them also with the charred remains of a post. This hole was 20 cm in diameter, 26 cm deep, and lined with small limestone cobbles; the other measured 17 cm in diameter and 24 cm deep.

Room 34 also contained four postholes, one in each corner of the room. They ranged from 15 cm to 20 cm in diameter and from 30 cm to 50 cm deep, and all were lined around the top with small cobbles and slabs. A section of charred post lay directly above the posthole in the southwest corner.

Evidence for a roof occurred as a layer of burned and unburned adobe chunks mixed with charcoal fragments, lying above the floor in each room. A few charred beams were also found in room 34. This layer produced the greatest amount of cultural material, including numerous pieces of ground stone and pottery vessels that might have been on the roof at the time it burned and collapsed. It also seems likely that these rooms served as trash dumps for some time after their abandonment.

Rooms 9 and 44. These small rooms, measuring 1.8 m by 2.0 m and 1.0 m by 1.4 m, respectively, were built on a layer of fill that had accumulated to a depth of 5–15 cm on the west side of rooms 11 and 12. There is a possibility that a third room once lay between the two, but no definite evidence for such a room was found.

Except for the foundation course of the west wall of room 9, which consisted of large limestone slabs placed vertically or horizontally on edge, the walls of both rooms were of horizontally placed slabs. These were generally evenly aligned on the interiors of the rooms, and a few slabs had been shaped by chipping. A gap of about 60 cm between the north and east walls of room 9 may have served as an entrance, and in room 44 there was no evidence that a south wall had ever existed. The east wall of room 9 was built partially above and beside what appeared to be part of an earlier wall. Remaining wall height was 10–46 cm, and no estimate of original height could be made.

In room 9, the fill on which the room was constructed had apparently been used unaltered as the floor. In room 44, a rough pavement of limestone slabs and cobbles had been laid unevenly on the surface of the fill. No evidence for a roof was found in either room.

A burial, feature 18, was found in room 9 and another, feature 25, in the area between rooms 9 and 44. The former was a young adult male whose grave goods consisted of five pottery vessels. Burial 25, a middle-aged male, was accompanied by three vessels. The burial pits for these individuals had been dug into the fill in and outside room 9; in the case of feature 18, the pit extended into the original clay ground surface.

Other features. The only well-defined use surface at GC212 was that associated with rooms 11, 12, 22, and 34. This surface was simply the naturally occurring clay overlying the limestone bedrock. Immediately south of room 11 was what appeared to be a pavement of closely spaced, drylaid limestone cobbles covering the original ground surface. The pavement was rather irregular because many of the cobbles were placed vertically or in a slanting position. The paved area extended about 2.5 m south of room 11 and measured about 2 m across.

A pit 50 cm in diameter and 54 cm deep was found during test excavations southeast of GC212; it contained a small ceramic bowl inverted over a small jar. The vessels were not identified by ware or type. In a series of test squares excavated in the area between GC212

152

and GC212A, six cists or borrow pits were located. All were basin shaped and unlined, and none contained cultural fill. They ranged from 40 cm to 1.75 m in diameter and from 7 cm to 28 cm deep.

A total of 25 roughly rectangular enclosures had been formed from fallen wall rubble above and outside of rooms 11, 12, 22, and 34. The rocks were arranged in irregular, drylaid alignments on a layer of fill about 20 cm thick above the roof fall layer in the rooms or the use surface outside. No well-defined use surface was observed at the level of the alignments, nor were any other features associated with them. The alignments appeared never to have been more than one course high. The function of the enclosures is uncertain, but it seems most likely that they represent the clearing of the abandoned site for agricultural plots.

GC212A

Room 62. Only the northern half of this room was excavated, but it appeared that all the existing walls were built of limestone slabs laid horizontally on the original ground surface. Some slabs in the north, east, and south walls had been shaped by chipping, and these walls generally had larger elements than did the west wall. No attempt had been made to align the slabs on either the interior or exterior of the room. Most of the east wall was missing. Remaining wall height was 4–40 cm, with four courses of stone standing in the north wall, one or two elsewhere. Little wall fall was found in the fill. Room 62 measured approximately 2.5 m by 5.4 m.

The floor appeared to be a layer of hard-packed earth 2–5 cm thick lying directly on the original ground surface. Across the north end of the room, a strip of floor about 50 cm wide was paved with small limestone and sandstone slabs. The room contained no interior features, but evidence for a roof was found in the form of a layer of burned chunks of adobe and sections of burned beams up to 12 cm in diameter that lay above the floor.

Rooms 39A and 39B. These small rooms, measuring about 2.1 m by 2.2 m and 2.4 m by 2.4 m, respectively, were built as a single structure with a dividing wall between them. All the walls were of limestone slabs placed horizontally in courses and chinked occasionally with small cobbles. The walls were laid directly on the original ground surface, and some of the slabs had been shaped by chipping. The southern ends of the east and west walls (in room 39A) were faced on the exterior by a second, parallel row of smaller slabs and cobbles. No attempt had been made to align the elements evenly on either side of the walls. Remaining wall height was 35–42 cm, and fallen elements would have brought the height to an estimated 60–95 cm.

In room 39A, an east-west dividing wall had been built of large, vertically placed slabs mortared to the floor in a single course. This wall or partition ended 70 cm short of the east wall.

The floors of both rooms consisted of a thin layer of hard-packed earth overlying the original ground surface. In a few places, the floor of room 39A seemed to have been constructed of wetlaid adobe. No evidence for a roof was found beyond a thin layer of burned adobe chunks on the floor of room 39A.

Two burial pits had been dug through the fill and to or into the floors of these rooms. Feature 46, an adult female buried in room 39A, was accompanied by eight pottery vessels. Feature 53, in room 39B, was a young adult female with five vessels and a bracelet of turquoise pendants and pipestone beads for grave accoutrements.

Other features. Extending northwest from room 39B was a wetlaid wall of limestone slabs set vertically into the original ground surface. It stood 20–60 cm high, and no additional slabs were found in the fill near the wall. However, a layer of burned chunks of adobe, some carrying beam impressions, lay on a use surface directly east of the wall. Associated with this use surface was an unlined, oval, basin-shaped fire pit measuring 86–111 cm in top diameter and 20 cm deep. It was filled with charcoal, burned adobe, and a number of burned limestone cobbles.

To the northeast of room 39B was an area of about 54 square meters covered with a layer of limestone cobbles and rocks over the original ground surface. The cobbles were rather loosely spaced and no more than one rock deep, and they did not actually constitute a pavement.

GC215

Site GC215 was located on "Sky Island," a pillar standing some 100 m from the rim of the Grand Canyon to the east of GC212. The top of the "island" was slightly more than 1 acre (0.5 hectare) in area, its vegetation predominantly piñon pine. Site GC215 comprised four linear roomblocks, the largest with seven rooms, the smallest with three, and the other two with four rooms each (Fig. 44). All the rooms were relatively small, the largest measuring 1.8 m by 4.9 m. Each roomblock had been built as a single unit with cross walls forming the individual rooms. Fifteen of the eighteen rooms were completely excavated and large areas outside them were stripped, revealing a well-defined use surface but few outlying features.

Roomblock A: Rooms 5, 4, 3, 2, 6, 7, 8

Although this roomblock was oriented with its long axis 35 degrees east of north, for purposes of description it will be considered oriented north-south with room 8 at the north end and room 5 at the south end. The east and west walls were continuous for the entire roomblock, except where the east wall had been dismantled and rebuilt to widen rooms 4 and 5. The foundation courses of both walls were set on or slightly into the original ground surface. Both were laid in generous amounts of adobe mortar and were usually well faced on the exterior. Some of the elements in their upper courses had been pecked to shape.

The foundation course of the east wall was of horizontally placed limestone blocks that decreased in size from north to south, and of smaller slabs in the vicinity of room 3. The upper courses of the east wall consisted of long, thin, limestone slabs except in the vicinity of room 7, where the upper wall was of variously sized blocks in no distinct courses. The remodeled portions of rooms 4 and 5 were of blocks set horizontally in a shallow foundation trench and chinked with pebbles and mortar.

The foundation course of the west wall was also of horizontally placed blocks that decreased in size from room 2 southward. The upper courses were mainly of small, horizontally laid blocks in the northern portion of the wall, grading into mixed blocks and slabs and then into horizontally placed slabs from room 2 south to room 5.

The cross walls of roomblock A all abutted the east and west walls except for the north wall of room 3, which had upper courses that interlocked with those of the east and west walls. The cross walls showed considerable variety in construction technique, no two being

155

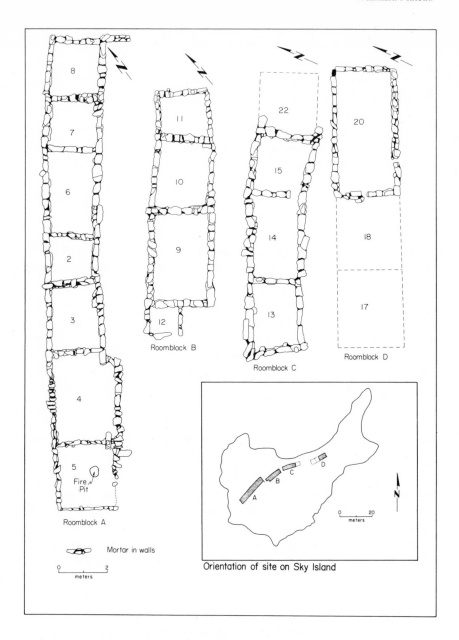

Roomblock B

Roomblock C

Roomblock D

Roomblock A

Mortar in walls

FIG. 44. Plan of site GC215.

156

exactly alike. Their foundation courses ranged from vertically set slabs to horizontally set blocks or combinations of blocks and slabs. In one case, the foundation was two rows wide. The upper courses also varied, ranging from small cobbles and irregular rocks to slabs and blocks that had been pecked to shape. Some walls were evenly faced, others were uneven. Mortar was used very generously in at least three of the walls.

Remaining wall height in roomblock A ranged from 7 cm to 65 cm, and fallen elements would have brought the height to an estimated 1.7 m. It is assumed that the walls were entirely of masonry up to the roof.

An above-ground entrance was visible in the wall fall east of room 6. Originally it must have stood about 60 cm above floor level and measured about 35 cm wide and 60 cm high. Another possible entrance was apparent, though less distinctly, in the wall fall east of room 8. Its outline was about 40 cm wide and 60 cm high, and it would have stood about 40 cm above the floor of the room. No other evidence for entrances was observed, but it seems reasonable to assume that the other rooms also opened toward the east.

All the floors in roomblock A consisted of a naturally occurring layer of clay that had been leveled off but otherwise was unaltered. Only room 5 contained a fire pit, which was unlined, circular, and basin shaped. It measured 55 cm in diameter and 20 cm deep and was filled with fine charcoal and a few fire-blackened cobbles. No evidence of a roof remained in any of the rooms.

The fill in all of the rooms consisted of about 25 cm of hard, clayey soil containing wall fall that was overlain by 5–20 cm of dark, uncompacted soil and pine duff. Only in room 6 was a distinct layer of trash noted directly above the floor, suggesting that this room was abandoned before the others. Three rooms produced assemblages of artifacts in floor contact: all or portions of six pots, two worked slabs, and a bone awl in room 5; a trough metate and four manos in room 4; and a trough metate, two manos, and a polishing stone in room 8. In room 7, a cache of four stone axes had been placed in the fill near the southwest corner.

Other features associated with roomblock A were two walls that extended at right angles from the east walls of rooms 6 and 8. Both were constructed from elements ranging from large blocks set horizontally on edge to smaller, horizontally placed slabs, and their remaining height was from 10 cm to 40 cm. The wall abutting room 6 was

L-shaped. Both walls were associated with the use surface outside the roomblock.

Roomblock B: Rooms 12, 9, 10, 11

This roomblock too was oriented northeast-southwest but for purposes of description will be treated as if it lay north-south, with room 12 to the south and room 11 on the north. The outside walls of rooms 9, 10, and 11 had all been constructed as a single unit with interlocking corners. The building elements varied somewhat in size and manner of placement, but in general all the walls were composed of limestone slabs laid horizontally in copious amounts of mortar on the original ground surface. The slabs in the east and south walls were somewhat more uniform in size than the others. All the walls were generally evenly faced, and 10 percent to 30 percent of the elements in the upper courses were pecked to shape.

The two cross walls forming rooms 9, 10, and 11 both abutted the east and west walls but differed considerably from each other. The wall between rooms 9 and 10 was of horizontally placed slabs and blocks, fairly evenly faced on both sides and set in thick layers of mortar. The second cross wall had a foundation course of nonuniform blocks and rough cobbles, usually set horizontally in thick mortar, and upper courses of more uniform blocks.

Room 12, at approximately 1 square meter the smallest room at the site, was built as an addition onto the south wall of room 9. The three new walls were of cobbles, blocks, and one long slab, with most of the elements placed horizontally. Only one course remained standing, and wall fall outside the room could not be distinguished from that of room 9. Throughout the entire roomblock, remaining wall height ranged from 12 cm to 53 cm, and the amount of wall fall inside and outside the rooms indicated that the walls were originally of masonry up to the roof.

The outline of an above-ground entrance was visible in the wall fall to the east of room 11; it measured 70 cm high and 40 cm wide and stood 40 cm above the floor of the room. In room 9, a shaped, rectangular schist slab that lay on the floor might have been a cover for a roof entry. The only possible indication of an entrance in room 12 was a 24-cm gap in the south wall at floor level.

In each room, the clay ground surface had been prepared by leveling and smoothing to serve as the floor. No evidence for roof construction was found in roomblock B. The fill in these rooms was identical to that in roomblock A, and there was no evidence of trash deposition. A metate, a mano, and all or portions of three pottery vessels were found lying on the floor of room 9.

Roomblock C: Rooms 13, 14, 15, 22

This roomblock, oriented with its long axis 72 degrees east of north, included four rooms of which three (rooms 13, 14 and 15) were excavated. The structure appeared to have been built as a single unit, although this could not be completely verified without the excavation of room 22.

The north wall of roomblock C was built of horizontally placed limestone blocks and slabs set directly on or slightly into the original ground surface. The building elements tended to decrease in size from west to east. The north wall interlocked with the west, which was also composed of horizontal blocks and slabs. The second course of both walls had slipped badly, so that its evenness could not be judged. The south wall of the roomblock was constructed from larger slabs and blocks, again set horizontally on the original ground surface. It was fairly well faced on both the interior and exterior, and moderately large amounts of mortar were used. About 15 percent of the upper course elements in the south wall showed evidence of pecking and battering, a higher percentage than for the other walls.

The cross walls dividing the roomblock abutted the north and south walls, except for the east wall of room 15 in which the third course interlocked with the north wall. All of the cross walls consisted of blocks or slabs or both laid horizontally on the original ground surface, but no two were constructed exactly alike. Remaining wall height throughout the roomblock ranged from 11 cm to 47 cm, and no estimate was made of original height.

The only suggestion of an entrance into any of the rooms was a shaped schist slab, possibly a doorway cover, that lay in the fill of room 15 near the south wall. A naturally occurring layer of clay underlying the roomblock had been used unaltered as the floor in each room. The only evidence of a roof found in any of the rooms was a thin layer of charred twigs and poles and chunks of beam-impressed adobe on the floor of room 13.

The fill of the rooms in roomblock C was identical to that already described for roomblocks A and B. Few major artifacts were found on the floor.

Roomblock D: Rooms 17, 18, 20

Roomblock D was oriented with its long axis 55 degrees east of north, but for description it will be considered oriented east-west. Although only room 20 was excavated, from the surface it appeared that this roomblock too had been built as a single unit. The east wall of room 20 abutted the south wall and was in turn abutted by the north wall, indicating that the long north and south walls of the roomblock were built simultaneously with the east wall.

The walls of room 20 appeared to have been constructed on the edges of a shallow pit that was cleared to an underlying layer of clay. The foundations of the walls were then set in a matrix of adobe and small pebbles. The north foundation consisted of very large limestone slabs set both vertically and horizontally on edge, with most of the elements unshaped. Only a few horizontally placed slabs remained of the upper courses of the north wall. The east wall had a foundation of one large block and a few smaller blocks and slabs that, like the upper courses of slabs, were laid horizontally in generous amounts of adobe mortar. The south wall was similar to the east but had smaller blocks in its foundation. The west wall had been almost entirely destroyed by root action. Remaining wall height was 4–76 cm, and fallen elements would have brought the walls to an estimated 1.9 m.

The bottom of the shallow excavation into the clay ground surface was used unaltered as the floor of room 20. There were no interior features and no evidence for a roof. Very little cultural material was found in the fill.

GC265

Site GC265 was located on a flat ridge in open ponderosa pine forest about 88 m north of GC268. The site included an L-shaped arrangement of four rooms, three of them contiguous in one linear roomblock and the fourth noncontiguous and oriented at right angles to the block (Fig. 45). Three of the rooms were excavated. To the south of the roomblock were three shallow depressions ranging from 2 m to 7 m in diameter. At first it was thought that these might be kivas, but testing showed that they extended only some 20 cm to bedrock. They may have been borrow pits where clay was quarried. Fairly extensive surface stripping was carried out to the east of the roomblock, but no features were encountered.

Rooms 2 and 4

These two excavated rooms each measured approximately 2 m by 4 m. Their walls were constructed of limestone slabs, most of which had been shaped by chipping and laid horizontally. Except for the north wall of room 4, which rested on a thin layer of mortar, the foundation courses lay on the original ground surface. The walls were evenly aligned on the exteriors of the rooms. Remaining wall height was 38–80 cm or from two to four courses high. It was estimated that fallen elements would have brought the original wall height to 1.5 m in room 2 and 2.0 m in room 4.

A possible floor-level entrance was located in the center of the east wall of room 2, where a gap 1 m wide had been sealed with small cobbles and adobe mortar. The floors of rooms 2 and 4 consisted of a layer of naturally occurring clay overlying bedrock, which apparently had been used without alteration. In room 4, this layer might have been covered by a 5-cm-thick layer of sand that was present in localized patches. In room 4, a 45-cm layer containing adobe chunks, some with beam impressions, and pieces of burned beams and poles lay over the floor and probably represented a burned roof. A layer of adobe chunks and small pieces of charcoal was the only possible evidence of the roof of room 2. Neither room contained any interior features or produced much cultural material.

Room 6

Room 6 measured about 3.0 m by 4.3 m and was not contiguous to the other rooms at GC265. The foundations of the north, east, and south walls were constructed of large, unshaped limestone slabs laid

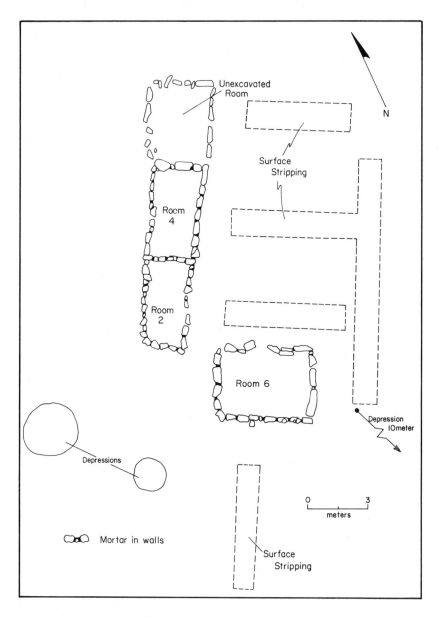

FIG. 45. Plan of site GC265.

vertically or horizontally on edge. The slabs were placed either directly on the original ground surface or on a thin layer of mortar. The entire west wall and the upper courses of the other walls were of smaller slabs partially shaped by chipping and laid horizontally. Except in the west wall, the elements varied considerably in size. All the walls were fairly evenly faced on both the interior and exterior. Remaining wall height was 40–70 cm, and although no estimate of original height could be made, it was noted that room 6 had less wall fall than the other rooms.

The clay layer overlying bedrock was apparently used unaltered as the floor of this room. No interior features were found, and only some adobe chunks and charred beams in the fill above the floor gave any indication of a roof. Room 6 also produced little cultural material.

SITES DATING AFTER A.D. 1050

GC264 (WP51)

Site GC264 was situated on a relatively flat ridge in open ponderosa pine forest about 75 m northwest of WP50. The site comprised at least two contiguous rooms oriented northeast to southwest. The northernmost room appeared to be larger than the other. As many as four alignments, 8 m long and 2–3 m apart, extended at right angles to the east of the roomblock. Two other alignments, 2 m long and 1 m apart, extended outward to the west of the northernmost room. The site was recorded during survey and a surface collection made, but it was not excavated.

GC269 (WP55, WP56)

Three separate rubble mounds were collectively assigned the number GC269 by Hall during his 1939 survey. Two of these were relocated by the SAR survey crew and numbered WP55 and WP56. Both were located on a flat ridgetop in open ponderosa pine forest, with WP55 lying about 45 m east of WP56. Neither site was excavated, but surface collections were made by both Hall and SAR.

WP55 was a mound of limestone cobbles, blocks, and slabs that measured 7 m by 15 m and was oriented almost exactly north-south. No room outlines were obvious from the surface, but one collapsed wall could be discerned. The size of the mound suggested that it contained two contiguous rooms.

WP56 was a similar mound of limestone blocks and slabs in which no wall outlines could be clearly observed. Measuring 5 m by 8 m, the mound probably comprised one or two rooms.

WP14

Site WP14 was located on a west-facing ridgetop in open ponderosa pine forest. It comprised a single masonry room and two or more drylaid rock alignments immediately north of the room (Fig. 46). The room was completely excavated. Test trenches and surface stripping outside the room revealed wall fall and midden to a depth of 15 cm, but no additional architectural features were found.

The room was nearly square, measuring approximately 2.7 m on a side. Its remaining walls stood no more than 35–57 cm high, but fallen elements would have brought them to an estimated 1.2 m. All foundation courses were built mainly of large limestone blocks set vertically either directly on the bedrock outcropping that formed the ridge or on a thin layer of adobe mortar. The upper courses were of smaller, horizontally laid limestone slabs. Even though the flat faces of the slabs were set inward, the interior faces of the walls were only slightly more evenly aligned than were the exteriors.

Where present, the thin layer of soil covering the bedrock was used without alteration as the floor of the room. In three areas, protruding bedrock had been pecked level with the floor surface. A semicircular subfloor cist was located along the west wall; it measured 35 cm in diameter and 15 cm deep and was filled with wall fall and sandy loam. A low "wall" of adobe, pebbles, and two limestone slabs extended 1 m into the room from the north wall. It stood only 12 cm high and 8 cm wide. No distinct roof fall was observed, and only a few small chunks of adobe in the fill provided possible evidence of a roof. Except for a few pieces of ground stone and a broken pot found on the floor, this room produced very little cultural material.

A roughly rectangular enclosure formed by drylaid alignments of limestone blocks adjoined the room to the north. A test trench exca-

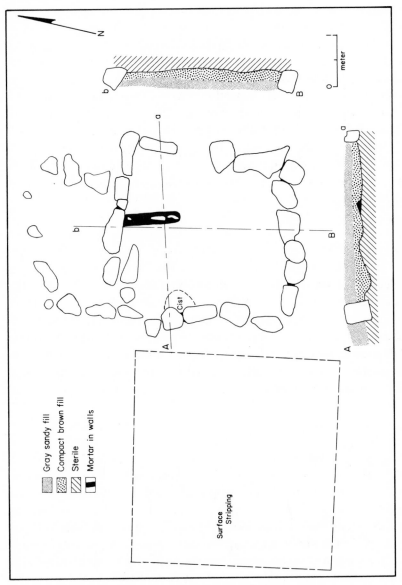

FIG. 46. Plan of site WP14.

Gray sandy fill
Compact brown fill
Sterile
Mortar in walls

N

meter

Surface
Stripping

Cist

165

vated along the westernmost alignment showed it to be resting on bedrock and revealed no associated features.

WP24

Site WP24 was located on a south-facing ridgetop roughly 350 m southeast of WP25. The surrounding biotic community is at present a transition between piñon-juniper and ponderosa pine forest. The site was a low, U-shaped mound of sparse rubble that opened to the north and seemed to comprise two or three contiguous, multiroomed structures. Only one room outline in the eastern wing of the site could be positively identified; it enclosed an area of about 8 square meters. A surface collection was made but no excavations were carried out.

WP34

Site WP34 was located on a ridge about 60 m from the rim of the Grand Canyon on the eastern edge of the Walhalla Plateau, and about 200 m north of WP33. The surrounding biotic community was open ponderosa pine forest. The site consisted of a single rectangular outline of limestone blocks and cobbles measuring some 9.5 m by 4.5 m. Only one course of rocks was visible, and no wall fall was observed. Only a surface collection was made.

WP37

Site WP37 was a rock overhang situated about one-fourth the way up a steep, east-facing slope in open ponderosa pine forest. The site itself was surrounded by small oak trees. The overhang covered an area 13 m long by 5 m deep and stood 2.1 m high above present ground level. Along the front edge of the overhang was a fallen masonry wall, and two walls had been constructed inside the shelter to divide it into three rooms. The roof of the overhang was smoke-blackened in several places.

A two-meter square was excavated in the center of the shelter, revealing culture-bearing fill to a depth of 50 cm. The front wall was found to have been constructed from 40 cm below the surface. It was composed of large, drylaid, vertically placed limestone blocks. No floor was recognizable in the test excavation, and no other features were found.

WP46

Site WP46 was located on a flat ridgetop in open ponderosa pine forest 25 m west of WP45. The site was a mound of limestone cobbles, blocks, and slabs measuring 9 m by 4 m and oriented almost exactly north-south. The outlines of at least five contiguous rooms could be seen in the rubble. A surface collection was made during survey, but the site was not excavated. WP46 may have been the same site as that numbered GC263A by Hall in 1938.

WP62

Site WP62 was located in the northern portion of the study area on a ridge above the drainage known as the Walhalla Glades. The surrounding vegetation was ponderosa pine. The site consisted of an alignment of drylaid boulders that ran down the slope of the ridge 12 m from west to east. A pile of similar boulders was located about 2 m south of the western end of the alignment. Although potsherds were scattered over the surface of the site, there was no good evidence for any rooms.

WP72

Site WP72 was located on a gentle, southeast-facing slope on the western edge of the Walhalla Plateau in the northern portion of the study area. It lay within 40 m of the rim of the Grand Canyon in open ponderosa pine forest with a few spruce trees. The site was composed of at least one masonry room, which was completely excavated (Fig. 47).

Measuring approximately 2 m by 2.9 m, the room had walls of limestone slabs laid horizontally directly on the original ground surface. In the south wall, only four slabs of the foundation course re-

FIG. 47. Site WP72, view to the south.

mained in place, and the other walls were one to two courses high. The slabs were unshaped, but where more than one course was present it appeared that the elements had been placed with flat faces toward the interior of the room. Very few slabs were found in the fill inside or outside the room.

The original ground surface was apparently used without alteration as the floor of WP72. No evidence of a roof or any interior features was found. A test pit excavated to the north of the northwest corner of the room produced fill and a use surface identical to that in the room, but it could not be determined whether another structure was present.

WP78

Site WP78 was a scatter of potsherds located north of the main study area, above the 8,200-foot contour line. The site was situated at the head of a small tributary ravine feeding into the Walhalla Glades drainage in a ponderosa pine-spruce-fir transition forest, with ponderosa predominating.

UNDATED SITES

GC276

Site GC276 was a rock overhang located halfway up a southwest-facing slope in open ponderosa pine forest about 300 m east of site WP36. The area sheltered by the overhang measured 39 m long by 12 m deep and 2 m high. A 2-m and a 1-m square were excavated near the center of the shelter, and culture-bearing fill was found to a depth of 40 cm. No hearths or architectural features were noted, although smoke stains were present in places on the roof.

GC326

Site GC326 was located near the base of an east-facing slope in open ponderosa pine forest roughly 120 m northwest of site WP22 and 30 m west of the Cape Royal road. The site was described by Hall as a single masonry room about 2 m on a side, but all that could be discerned on the surface during the SAR survey were a few limestone blocks and cobbles with no definite orientation. Two test pits were excavated and culture-bearing fill was found in one of them to a depth of 40 cm. No architectural or other features were encountered. It is possible that some other site in the near vicinity was actually Hall's GC326.

WP2

This site designation was given to three large bifaces found within a 50-m radius of site WP22.

WP3

This site designation was given to a large chert biface found in the vicinity of Greenland Lake, north of the main study area.

WP4

This site designation was given to a large, unnotched biface found 50 m north of Greenland Lake.

WP5

Site WP5 was located on a low ridge 70 m northeast of Greenland Lake, a sinkhole that has been made into a collecting tank through the construction of an earth dam on its downhill side. Situated in a mixed ponderosa pine, fir, and aspen forest, the "lake" held standing water during the 1969 and 1970 summer field seasons.

WP5 was a concentration of chipped stone artifacts scattered over an area some 120 m in diameter. Twenty to thirty percent of the site area was stripped to a depth of 10 cm, where culturally sterile soil was encountered, and all fill was screened. A few potsherds were recovered in addition to the stone artifacts, indicating the presence of Pueblo people between A.D. 1050 and 1150. However, the lithic assemblage from WP5 was decidedly unlike those found elsewhere on the Walhalla Plateau and is discussed in more detail in Chapter 5.

WP6

Site WP6 was a scatter of chipped stone artifacts found over an area about 15 m in diameter. It was located 60 m east-southeast of Greenland Lake on a west-facing slope.

WP7–11

The site designations WP7 through WP11 were assigned to five pictographs or clusters of pictographs (Fig. 48) located below the rim of the Grand Canyon east of GC212. These pictographs had been discovered by Harvey Butchart, who personally led the SAR survey team to them. They were situated at elevations from 10 m to 100 m below the canyon rim, all in places that were protected from rainfall or surface runoff. The paintings had been executed in red pigments and in one case (WP9) white pigment on the smooth vertical face of the Kaibab limestone. The paint had been applied either with the fingers— some of the pictographs were hand prints—or with a brush.

WP12

Site WP12 was located roughly 250 m northeast of GC212 and 40 m east of the present Cape Royal road. It was situated on a north-facing slope in open ponderosa pine forest. The site consisted of a roughly

FIG. 48. Petroglyphs on the cliff face below the southeast edge of the Walhalla Glades. Top: site WP8. Bottom: site WP9.

rectangular outline of limestone blocks and slabs measuring about 3.5 m by 2.7 m and oriented northeast-southwest. It was uncertain whether the alignments represented a room or a few agricultural terraces. A small surface collection was made but no excavations were carried out.

WP13

Site WP13 was situated near the bottom of an east-facing slope about 150 m northeast of GC212, on the east side of the Cape Royal road. The plant community in the vicinity was open ponderosa pine forest. The site consisted of a single alignment of limestone cobbles and boulders 5.6 m long running parallel to the contours of the slope. This feature may have been an agricultural terrace. A few lithic artifacts were scattered over the site surface but no ceramics were found.

WP15

Site WP15 was located on a ridgetop in open ponderosa pine forest 17 m north of WP14. It consisted of a low, L-shaped mound of small limestone rocks with a roughly circular depression about 5 m in diameter between the two arms. The mound probably comprised three rooms, and the outline of a fourth small room could be seen 10 m northeast of the roomblock. A test trench was excavated in the depression, but culturally sterile soil was reached at a depth of 30 cm, and there appeared to be no structure present.

WP16

Site WP16, which might have been Hall's GC259, was situated on a ridgetop in open ponderosa pine forest about 110 m north of WP15 and 10 m west of the present Cape Royal road. The site was a rectangular outline of blocks and cobbles measuring roughly 5.5 m by 3.5 m and oriented with its long axis 10 degrees west of north. A few lithic artifacts but no sherds were found on the surface.

WP17

Site WP17 was located at the top of a steep, north-facing slope on the west side of the Cape Royal road, 33 m southwest of WP16. The present biotic community in the area is open ponderosa pine forest. WP17 comprised a rectangular outline of blocks, presumably a room, and a series of three parallel alignments. The room measured approximately 2 m by 3 m and was oriented about 10 degrees east of north. The alignments, situated downslope from the room and running parallel to the contours of the slope, ranged from 2.4 m to 3.7 m long and were spaced from 35 cm to 80 cm apart. A small surface collection was made.

WP18

Site WP18 (Fig. 49) was a single room situated at the bottom of a north-facing slope in open ponderosa pine forest. It lay 80 m west of the Cape Royal road and 900 m north of GC212 (54 m northeast of

FIG. 49. Site WP18, view to the west. Note fire pit near west wall.

WP19). The room, which was the only architectural feature noticed at the site, was excavated and found to measure roughly 2.2 m by 2.5 m, its long axis oriented north-south.

The walls of the room were constructed of limestone blocks and slabs. In the east, west, and south walls, these were set vertically or horizontally on edge, either slightly into the original ground surface or mortared to it. The north wall consisted of horizontally placed blocks. Nearly all the building elements showed evidence of shaping by pecking, and all the walls were more evenly faced on the interior than on the exterior. Fallen sections of the walls in the fill indicated that all upper courses had consisted of horizontally placed slabs smaller than those of the foundations. Remaining wall height was 20–100 cm, and fallen elements would have brought the walls no higher than the highest standing sections.

The original ground surface of decomposed limestone was used without alteration as the floor of the room. A circular fire pit 65 cm in diameter and 10 cm deep lay midway along the west wall. It was lined with thin sandstone slabs and filled with sandy loam. No good evidence of a roof could be found, but a short section of a burned beam 10 cm in diameter lay on the floor and might have been part of a roof beam. The room produced very little cultural material.

WP19

Site WP19 was a series of two or three alignments of cobbles and blocks situated near the bottom of an east-facing slope 54 m southwest of WP18. The alignments measured about 30 m long and lay 2–3 m apart, running parallel to the contours of the slope. Very little artifactual material was found on the site surface.

Immediately upslope from the alignments was evidence that a modern, temporary camp had been made by leveling surfaces into the side of the slope. Baling wire and tin cans were found in association with these "terraces," which probably had been used by recent road construction crews.

WP20

Site WP20, a series of probable agricultural terraces, was located on the lower portion of a rather steep, west-facing slope 120 m southeast of WP19. At least four parallel alignments of drylaid cobbles and blocks were visible (Fig. 50), running parallel to the contours of the slope. They ranged from 7 m to 11 m in length and were spaced at 2 m to 5 m intervals. A test trench excavated through three of the terraces showed that each alignment held back as much as 25 cm of soil. Very little artifactual material was found either on the site surface or in the test trench.

WP21

Site WP21 was situated on the upper portion of a rather steep, north-facing slope 23 m northeast of WP20 in open ponderosa pine forest. The site consisted of a nearly square outline of limestone cobbles and blocks measuring 2.3 m by 2.2 m. A few lithic artifacts but no potsherds were found on the site surface.

WP22

Site WP22, a scatter of lithic artifacts and potsherds covering an area about 14 m in diameter, was located near the rim of the Grand Canyon 66 m northeast of WP23. The site was tested by stripping 13 2-meter squares to a depth of about 6 cm, at which culturally sterile soil was encountered. Surface collections were made from an additional two 2-meter squares. No architectural features were found, and too few sherds were recovered to allow confident dating of the site.

WP23

Site WP23 was located on a nearly level bench halfway down a gentle, west-facing slope 66 m southwest of WP22. It consisted of a rectangular outline of cobbles and blocks measuring about 4 m by 4.5 m, with its long axis oriented due east-west. Very little cultural material was found on the site surface.

WP25

WP25 was a single alignment of blocks and slabs located on a relatively flat ridgetop 55 m northwest of WP24. It measured 3.2 m long, was oriented 40 degrees west of north, and did not seem to be

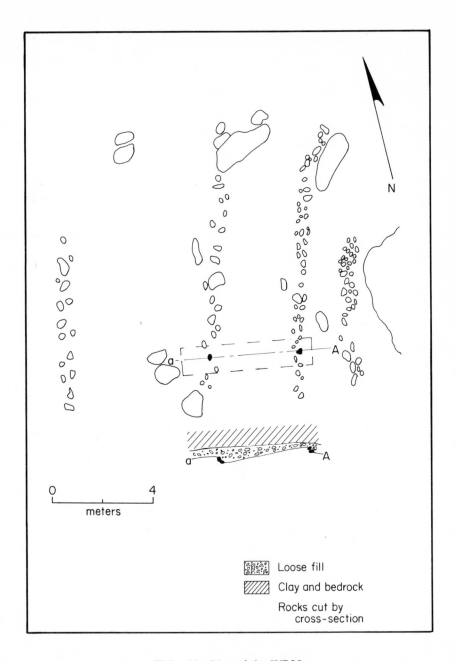

N

0   4

meters

Loose fill

Clay and bedrock

Rocks cut by
   cross-section

FIG. 50. Plan of site WP20.

part of a room. No artifactual material was found on the ground surface in the vicinity of the alignment.

WP26

Site WP26 was located near the top of a west-facing slope about 250 m northwest of WP25 in open ponderosa pine forest. The site consisted of two alignments of rocks about 1 m apart and running parallel to the contours of the slope. They measured 2 m and 3 m long. No cultural material was found on the site surface.

WP27

Site WP27 was situated on a south-facing slope 10 m due west of WP26. The site designation was given to a series of at least five check dams formed by alignments of cobbles and boulders extending across a small drainage. Five such alignments were recorded, but as many as six more existed downstream. No cultural material was found on the site surface.

WP28

Site WP28 was located on an east-facing ridgetop about 75 m northeast of WP30. The site consisted of two rectangular cobble outlines about 8 m apart, presumably representing rooms. One outline measured about 3 m by 4.2 m, the other roughly 3 m on a side. No cultural material was found on the site surface.

WP29

WP29 was the designation given to a fragment of a large thinned biface found 100 m north of WP28.

WP30

Site WP30 was situated on a slightly south-facing ridgetop 60 m northwest of WP31 in open ponderosa pine forest. The site consisted of a cobble-and-block room outline measuring 2 m by 3 m, with its long axis oriented about 30 degrees east of north. Very little cultural material was found on the surface.

WP31

Site WP31 was located on a flat ridge about 60 m southeast of WP30 in open ponderosa pine forest. The site was a mound of cobbles and blocks in which the definite outline of at least one room was visible. This room measured 1.9 m by 2.3 m and was oriented about 10 degrees west of north. Very little artifactual material was found on the site surface.

WP32

Site WP32 was located near the edge of a slightly east-facing ridgetop 75 m southeast of WP31. The site comprised two cobble-and-block alignments 9.3 m and 10.2 m long and 2.5 m apart, oriented parallel with the contours of the slope. No surface material was found.

WP33

Site WP33 was located north of Cape Final on a west-facing slope about 220 m southwest of WP34. The site was a three-sided outline of cobbles and blocks about 2 m on a side. It produced no surface material.

WP35

Site WP35 was situated about halfway down a steep, west-facing slope 150 m southwest of GC212. It consisted of a vague, cobble-and-block outline measuring 4 m by 2.5 m and presumably representing a room. No surface material was found.

WP36

Site WP36 was a circular depression 8 m in diameter and partially ringed with limestone rubble. It lay on a gently sloping, northwest-facing ridgetop roughly 80 m northwest of WP21 in open ponderosa pine forest. Two test trenches yielded trash fill to a depth of 42 cm, but no walls or floor was encountered. The few sherds recovered did not allow definite dating of the site.

WP38

Site WP38 was located on a ledge halfway down an east-facing slope directly above WP37. It consisted of a U-shaped mound of cobble-and-block rubble measuring 3 m by 4.6 m and opening toward the bottom of the slope. A very small surface collection was made.

WP39

Site WP39 was situated on an east-facing ridgetop 50 m southwest of WP44 in open ponderosa pine forest. The site was a low mound of cobbles and blocks measuring about 3.5 m by 4 m. No definite wall outlines were observed, and no cultural material was found on the site surface.

WP40

Site WP40 was a three-sided rubble outline measuring 3.6 m by 5 m, with its long axis oriented almost exactly north-south. It was located about 40 m southwest of WP28 on a ridgetop sloping gently to the south. Very little surface material was available for collection.

WP41

Site WP41 was located on a ridgetop sloping slightly to the south, in open ponderosa pine forest in the southwest portion of the Walhalla Plateau. It consisted of a 4 m by 9 m mound of limestone cobbles and blocks in which the outlines of two contiguous rooms could be seen. A small amount of cultural material was found on the site surface.

WP43

Site WP43 was located about 50 m southeast of WP41, on the same ridgetop. This site included a mound of cobbles and blocks some 7.5 m by 16 m. It was covered by an oak thicket, and no clear room outlines

179

were discernible. Directly south of the mound was a sherd concentration, but the ceramic collection did not allow dating of the site.

WP44

Site WP44 was situated near the top of a southeast-facing slope 50 m northeast of WP39 in the ponderosa pine community. It comprised the cobble-and-slab outlines of two noncontiguous rooms about 10 m apart, one measuring 2.5 m by 3.2 m and the other 2.2 m by 5.6 m. Both were oriented with their long axes parallel to the contours of the slope or about 15 degrees east of north. No potsherds were found on the site surface.

WP45

Site WP45 was a crescent-shaped pile of limestone cobbles located 25 m east of WP46 on a ridgetop sloping gently to the east. The crescent opened to the north and measured 1.4 m by 2.7 m. It did not seem to be the remains of a room. No artifacts were found on the site surface.

WP47

Site WP47 was located on a relatively flat ridgetop 20 m southwest of WP46 in open ponderosa pine forest. The site consisted of two mounds of cobble-and-block rubble situated 2 m apart and a room outline visible 2 m north of the northernmost rubble pile. The room outline measured about 2 m on a side, the mounds about the same. Adjacent to the northernmost mound was a depression some 4 m by 6 m. Very little cultural material was found on the site surface.

WP48

Site WP48, located on a relatively flat ridgetop 58 m northeast of WP46, was a jumbled pile of limestone slabs and blocks measuring 7.2 m by 2.3 m by 0.7 m high. Many of the rocks stood on edge or at an angle to horizontal, in contrast to those in nearly all the collapsed rooms encountered during the survey. The site might have been a pile of rocks gathered for building purposes but never used. No artifactual material was found on the surface.

WP49

Site WP49 was a one-room outline of horizontally placed slabs, 2.3 m on a side. It was situated on a relatively flat ridgetop 67 m northwest of WP46. Very little surface material was found.

WP50

Site WP50 was located on a relatively flat ridgetop 100 m northwest of WP46. The site consisted of an L-shaped mound of slabs and blocks within which three room outlines were visible. The long arm of the L was oriented to the northwest, and the rooms averaged 2.5 m by 2.2 m. A few sherds and lithic artifacts were found on the site surface.

WP53

The designation WP53 was given to a series of at least nine agricultural terraces located along the northern edge of the ridge on which sites GC265, GC268, and GC270 were also found. The terraces averaged 2.5 m wide and were bounded by alignments of drylaid cobbles and slabs stacked up to 25 cm high in rows running parallel to the contours of the hill. The maximum length of the terraces was 300 m, but the alignments were not continuous over this entire distance. A test trench excavated across four of the terraces showed that the soil behind them averaged 20 cm deep. Little cultural material was found either on the site surface or in the test trench.

WP57

Site WP57 was located in the northern portion of the study area, north of Cape Final, on a west-facing ridge above the Walhalla Glades drainage. The site consisted of four or five alignments of cobbles and

181

blocks averaging 12 m long and spaced 1.1 m apart. They were oriented parallel to the contours of the slope and probably functioned as agricultural facilities. No cultural material was found on the site surface.

WP58

Site WP58, situated on the same ridge and about 100 m southwest of WP57, was an L-shaped rubble alignment that may have been a room. Some of the slabs making up the alignment were set vertically, and the outline measured 2.5 m by 2.7 m. Very little surface material was found.

WP59

Site WP59 was the designation given to two cobble-and-block alignments located near the bottom of a fairly steep, east-facing slope 175 m west of WP58. The alignments, presumably agricultural terraces, measured 5 m and 7 m long, were spaced 1.3 m apart, and ran parallel to the contours of the slope. No surface artifacts were found.

WP60

Site WP60 was located north of Cape Final on a relatively flat ridgetop about 100 m northeast of WP59, in open ponderosa pine forest. The site consisted of a single mound of cobbles, slabs, and blocks, measuring 8 m by about 3.5 m, with its long axis oriented northeast-southwest. Portions of a fallen wall were observed along one side of the mound, but no definite room outlines were visible. A small surface collection was made.

WP61

Site WP61 was located in the northern part of the study area roughly 125 m southeast of WP63. It lay near the top of an east-facing slope in ponderosa pine forest with some spruce trees. The site was a low mound of cobbles scattered over an area about 3 m by 5 m. Its long axis was oriented about 25 degrees east of north. Too few sherds were found on the site surface to permit dating of the site.

WP63

Site WP63 was located near the top of an east-facing slope 45 m northwest of WP62. It comprised a U-shaped mound of cobbles and slabs that opened toward the bottom of the slope and measured 3.2 m by 4 m. A very small surface collection was made.

WP64

Although its exact location was not recorded, site WP64 lay somewhere north of the main study area in the narrow neck of land that joins the Walhalla Glades area to the rest of the Walhalla Plateau. The site was a U-shaped outline of limestone cobbles and blocks, open to the west and measuring 2 m by 2.2 m. No surface material was found.

WP65

Site WP65 was located in the same general vicinity as WP64. It consisted of a scatter of cobbles and blocks in no recognizable pattern. Virtually no surface material was found.

WP66

Site WP66 was not recorded on the survey map, but it was described as lying north of Cape Final on a ridgetop 25 m west of the Cape Royal road and about 5.1 km north along that road from site GC212. The site, measuring 9 m on each side, was a low mound of cobbles, slabs, and blocks. No room outlines were apparent from the surface, and little cultural material was found.

WP67

Site WP67 was situated at the eastern edge of a ridgetop in open ponderosa pine forest about 40 m west of the Cape Royal road and some 7 km along that road north of GC212. The site comprised two noncontiguous rooms about 8 m apart and a circular depression 5 m in diameter lying to the southeast of the rooms. A test trench was excavated through the center of the depression; but no architectural features could be defined, and the fill was culturally almost sterile. A surface collection was also made but was insufficient to allow dating of the site.

WP68

The exact location of site WP68 was not recorded, but it too lay somewhere to the north of the study area proper in the narrow neck of land joining the Walhalla Glades area to the rest of the Walhalla Plateau. The site was situated near the top of a northeast-facing slope near the rim of the Grand Canyon and consisted of a single cobble-and-boulder alignment built across a small drainage channel. It measured 4.5 m long and presumably served as a check dam. No surface material was found.

WP69

Site WP69 was located somewhere in the general vicinity of WP68 and other sites whose exact locations were not recorded during survey. It lay on a west-sloping ridgetop in a ponderosa pine-fir-aspen forest. WP69 was a low mound of cobbles, slabs, and blocks measuring 2 m by 2.8 m. No wall outlines could be discerned from the surface, and no artifactual material was found.

WP70

The designation WP70 was given to three lithic artifacts and a single potsherd found far to the northwest of the Walhalla Glades in the vicinity of Upper Thompson Spring, just west of Arizona State Road 67 at about 8,300 feet in elevation. The artifacts were found in a spruce-fir forest overlooking a meadow.

WP79

Site WP79 was located at about 8,300 feet and was north of the main study area and midway down an east-facing slope in mixed ponderosa pine-fir-spruce forest. The site was a single rectangular outline of unshaped blocks measuring 2 m by 2.6 m. A small surface collection was made.

WP80

Site WP80, located about 200 m south of WP79, was a rubble mound measuring about 3 m by 6 m. It had no distinct alignments. The site was situated halfway up an east-facing slope in ponderosa pine-spruce-fir forest at about 8,200 feet.

WP81

Located about 300 m south of site WP80, the rubble mound designated as WP81 lay on an east-sloping ridgetop in a predominantly ponderosa pine forest at about 8,180 feet. The mound measured some 5 m by 3 m and had no distinct room outlines.

WP82

Site WP82, located slightly over 1 km south of WP81, was a fairly distinct, rectangular rock outline probably representing a single room. It was situated on an east-facing slope in ponderosa pine forest with a few spruce trees, at about 8,100 feet in elevation.

KP1

Site KP1 was located on the Kaibab Plateau far from the main study area, near Grand Canyon Lodge. It lay on a ridgetop along the Transept Trail, 15 m from the rim of the Grand Canyon. The site appeared to consist of a single masonry room, which was completely excavated (Fig. 51). No tests were made for other architectural features.

The excavated room was a long rectangle measuring 1.9 m by 6.9 m; these dimensions suggest that the structure might once have been divided by a cross wall, though no good evidence for one was found. The foundation courses of the east and west walls were built of large limestone blocks placed horizontally on edge, while the upper courses

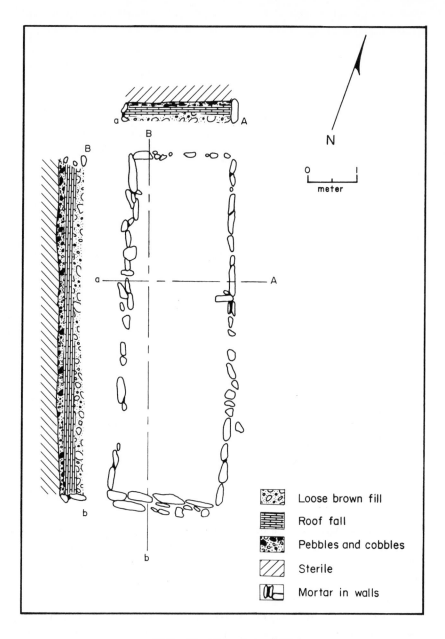

FIG. 51. Plan of site KP1.

were of smaller blocks laid horizontally. The north and south wall foundations were of adobe mortar mixed with large pebbles, and the upper courses consisted of horizontally placed blocks and cobbles. The east and west walls were more evenly aligned on the interior than were the north and south walls. Remaining wall height was 35–50 cm, and fallen elements would have brought the walls only to an estimated 65 cm.

The floor of the room was a 2–3 cm layer of sandy adobe with inclusions of small pebbles, laid directly on the original ground surface. A 12-cm layer of fill containing chunks of adobe and pieces of charcoal was the only possible evidence of a roof. The room produced very little cultural material.

SITES LOCATED ON WOTAN'S THRONE

WT1

Site WT1 was a scatter of lithic artifacts over an area of about 0.2 ha on a south-facing slope. The material included a blade fragment and a number of chert flakes.

WT2

Site WT2 (Fig. 52) was a single rectangular room measuring 1.8 m by 2.7 m and oriented with its long axis 30 degrees east of north. Test excavations in the southeast corner of the room showed that the walls were constructed of drylaid, horizontally placed limestone cobbles and blocks. In a few cases the foundation elements had been placed vertically. Remaining wall height ranged from a few centimeters to 73 cm, and wall fall inside and outside the room would have brought the walls to an estimated 1 m.

The walls had been built directly on the clay that overlaid the Kaibab limestone, a natural layer that was used unaltered as the floor. A concentration of charcoal chunks and ash in the southeast corner might have indicated a hearth area, but no actual fire pit was present. A cluster of sherds from a Moenkopi Corrugated pot lay on the floor near

FIG. 52. Site WT2 on Wotan's Throne.

the charcoal concentration. No evidence of a roof was found, and the general character of the room suggested that it had not seen a very long occupation.

WT3

Site WT3 was situated about 6 m below the rim of Wotan's Throne, in a low overhang. It consisted of two wetlaid walls extending from the front to the rear of the shelter, forming a sort of open room 1.1 m long, 1 m deep, and 70 cm high. The walls were constructed of unshaped, horizontally placed blocks and slabs. Some indications of mortar were noticed on the floor along the front of the overhang, suggesting that a wall might once have stood there to fully enclose the room. No artifactual material was found in the vicinity of the structure.

WT4

Site WT4 was a possible granary located in an overhang immediately west of WT3. No further description is available.

WT5

Site WT5 was a three-sided rock outline, presumably of a room, measuring roughly 1.2 m by 1.9 m and oriented with its long axis 30 degrees west of north. The east wall was missing, but the others were constructed of unshaped, drylaid limestone blocks and slabs that stood no more than two courses high. No surface material was found.

WT6

Site WT6 was a semicircle of drylaid limestone blocks, cobbles, and slabs with a radius of 1 m, its open side toward the east. No cultural material was found in its vicinity.

WT7

Site WT7 (Fig. 53) was a stone wall almost 3 m long situated on the east edge of Wotan's Throne, about 1 m from the rim itself. In places the wall, composed of limestone blocks and slabs, stood as much as 11 courses high.

FIG. 53. Site WT7 on Wotan's Throne.

WT8

The designation WT8 was given to 13 sherds from a Shinarump Corrugated pot.

WT9

Site WT9 (Fig. 54) appeared to be one or two small agricultural terraces bounded by rock alignments measuring 5 m and 15 m long and spaced 1.5 m apart.

WT10

Site WT10 (Fig. 55) was a roughly square room measuring approximately 2.5 m on a side. Its walls were built mainly of unshaped, drylaid limestone slabs. They stood from 50 cm to 80 cm high, and a considerable amount of wall fall was visible inside and outside the structure. A shallow trough metate lay on the ground 2 m east of the room, and other cultural material was collected from the surface.

FIG. 54. Site WT9, probable agricultural terraces on Wotan's Throne.

FIG. 55. Site WT10 on Wotan's Throne.

Appendix B

HUMAN SKELETAL REMAINS

The remains of four human skeletons were found during excavation in the Walhalla Glades, all of them primary interments at site GC212/212A. Two adult males, one middle aged and one younger, had been buried in the portion of the site designated GC212, and two females of about the same ages as the males were found in roomblock GC212A (Fig. 56). Each body had been placed on its right side in a semiflexed position for burial. The older individuals were positioned with their heads to the west, the younger ones with their heads to the north or northwest. Three of the individuals had been laid in shallow pits dug through the floors of rooms 9, 39A, and 39B, and the fourth was buried in the fill outside room 9. The stratigraphic evidence indicated that the interments had all been made at or very close to the same time, and together they were likely the final event taking place before abandonment of the site.

All of the burials were accompanied by grave goods, which ranged from three to eight pottery vessels and included one bracelet of shale and turquoise beads. The pots included both jars and bowls in a variety of sizes, forms, and ceramic types. They usually were arranged in clusters at the head or feet of the individual, or in both places. Bowls

FIG. 56. Four burials found at site GC212/212A. Clockwise from upper left:
burial 18, burial 25, burial 46, burial 53.

were commonly placed in an inverted position, often covering the mouths of jars. For more details on the pottery of the mortuary assemblages, the reader is referred to Chapter 4.

Two of the skeletons were extremely fragmentary, but the other two were fairly complete and in fair to excellent condition. Three skulls complete enough for analysis exhibited intentional deformation of the parietals and occipital, a common type of Pueblo cranial deformation known as lambdoid flattening (Reed 1949). Dental pathologies were common and included premortem tooth loss, caries, abscesses, and periodontal disease. The older male also had widespread osteoarthritis.

In the following descriptions of the burials, information about age, sex, skeletal condition, and pathologies was provided by Peter L. Eidenbach, who analyzed the skeletal remains. The pottery types

194

found in the mortuary assemblages were identified by Michael P. Marshall.

BURIAL GC212-18

The individual assigned feature number 18 was a young adult male, possibly about age 25. The skeleton was extremely fragmentary with only portions of the skull, pelvis, and legs remaining, although the few bones present were generally in fair condition. The individual's age was estimated on the basis of evidence showing that all epiphyses present were fused, whereas the coronal suture was unfused. Evidence that the individual was a male included the presence of a large auricular surface, the lack of a preauricular sulcus, the narrow sciatic notch of the pelvis, and the 48-mm transverse diameter of the head of the femur.

Burial 18 was placed in a pit dug through the floor of room 9 and into the underlying red clay. Because the floor was simply the surface of the fill on which the room was built, the pit could not be clearly defined above the clay layer; however, it probably measured about 1.5 m by 90 cm. The individual was placed semiflexed on his right side, with his head to the north.

Five pottery vessels accompanied this individual in the grave (see Fig. 30): two bowls identified as Walhalla White Ware and Cameron or Citadel Polychrome, and three jars identified as Tusayan Black-on-red, Shinarump Corrugated, and either Sosi Black-on-white or Flagstaff Black-on-white. The Shinarump Corrugated vessel lay next to the skull, the other vessels in the vicinity of the feet. The Cameron/Citadel Polychrome bowl, of which only about half was present, was inverted over the mouth of the Tusayan Black-on-red jar, and both exhibited a calcium carbonate patina probably resulting from the evaporation of water from the jar.

BURIAL GC212-25

This burial, located immediately south of room 9, was a mature male probably between the ages of 35 and 50. Although the left side of the pelvis and the entire left leg and foot were missing, the rest of the skeleton was present in good to excellent condition. The age estimate was based on the great degree of dental attrition evident, the fusion of all epiphyses, extensive cranial suture closure, and medium to extensive osteoarthritic lipping of the vertebrae. Evidence for male sex was based on the pelvis, skull, mandible, and femur, as follows:

Pelvis: large, oval obturator foramen, large acetabulum, narrow sciatic notch, large sacrum-ilium articulation, lack of preauricular sulcus, sacrum with wide base and moderate curvature;

Skull: marked brow ridges, large, distinct mastoid, marked posterior root of zygomatic process;

Mandible: large, chin somewhat square;

Femur: transverse diameter of head 52 mm.

The completeness of the skeleton allowed an estimate of stature to be calculated using the formula for the "Mongoloid" type of Trotter and Gleser (1958). The individual was estimated to have been 162.1 cm tall, plus or minus 3.18 cm; that is, 63.8 inches. He suffered from osteoarthritis, particularly in the right hip, the right shoulder, and the lumbar region of the spine. Periodontal disease was indicated by extensive resorption of the alveolar portions of the maxilla and mandible. The individual had lost all but five of his teeth prior to death and had advanced caries in one remaining premolar.

Burial 25 had been placed on his right side with his head to the west, in a semiflexed position. His shallow grave had been dug out of the fill that had accumulated above the original clay ground surface outside room 9, but it did not extend all the way to that surface. Although the burial pit could not be completely delineated in the soft fill, it measured at least 1.1 m by 75 cm. Since the surface of this fill was the same level that served as the floor of room 9, we assume that the two interments were made simultaneously.

Accompanying the skeleton were three ceramic vessels identified as a Walhalla White Ware bowl, a Walhalla Corrugated jar, and the bowl portion of a Flagstaff Black-on-white ladle (see Fig. 31). A large Middleton Polychrome sherd that might have served as a jar lid was

196

also found in the burial pit. All of these vessels lay in front of the face of the skeleton.

BURIAL GC212A-46

Burial 46 was probably a female about 35 to 45 years old. She had been placed in a pit dug into the floor of room 39A in roomblock GC212A. The pit was clearly defined in the floor and measured 1.3 m long by 90 cm wide. Most of the skeleton had been destroyed by the roots of nearby trees, and the remaining bones were badly eroded and crushed. However, it was clear that this individual had been buried in a semiflexed position on her right side, with her head to the west and facing south.

Evidence for the sex of the individual was the small size of the skull vault, the small mastoid, and the slight extension of the posterior zygomatic root. The age estimate was based on the complete closure of the coronal suture, the extensive closure of the lambdoid suture, and dental attrition. No complete analysis of the dentition was possible due to the absence of the maxilla and the erosion of the mandible. However, at least five teeth had been lost premortem, and extensive resorption of the alveolar portion of the mandible was visible.

Two clusters of pots had been placed with burial 46 (see Fig. 32), one group of three just beyond the head and the other of six vessels around the feet and lower legs. Vessels in the former group were a large Flagstaff Black-on-white bowl and a small one that rested on top of a small Tusayan Corrugated jar. In the cluster at the feet of the burial were a Dogoszhi Black-on-white jar, a Sosi Black-on-white jar, a Walnut Black-on-white bowl inverted over a Tusayan Black-on-red jar, and a second such bowl inverted over the neck portion of a Shinarump Corrugated jar.

A mano fragment was also found in the burial pit near the feet of the skeleton and could have been either a mortuary offering or simply some trash included in the pit fill. Similarly, a metate that rested upright against the wall of the room, beyond the feet of the individual, may or may not have been part of the grave accoutrements. It lay at floor level above and outside the recognizable burial pit, but the vessels at the head of the skeleton lay in the same stratigraphic relationship to the pit. The positions of these artifacts suggest that the interment was made just prior to the room's abandonment, when the floor was still exposed and no fill had yet accumulated.

BURIAL GC212A-53

Burial 53 lay in a shallow, irregularly shaped pit in the floor of room 39B. The individual was most likely a young adult female, possibly between 20 and 25 years of age. This age assessment was based on tooth loss and wear and on suture closure. Her sex was indicated by the generally small size of the skeleton, particularly the skull and mandible. Other evidence included the slight brow ridges, a small mastoid, a slight posterior extension of the zygomatic root, and, with respect to the pelvis, a wide sciatic notch and an obturator foramen that was triangular in outline. The skeleton was in fair condition, the hands and feet entirely eroded away but most other body parts represented to some degree.

Although parts of the mandible and maxilla were missing, the remaining portions exhibited several pathologies. Three teeth had dental caries, in one case extremely advanced, and two dental abscesses were also noted, one small and one major. At least one tooth had been lost premortem.

This individual had been placed on her right side in a semiflexed position, her head to the northwest. In front of the face were three pottery vessels: a small Holbrook Black-on-white bowl, a large Flagstaff Black-on-white bowl, and a large Walnut Black-on-white seed jar. These lay on the floor just outside the burial pit, their positions suggesting that they had originally been stacked one on another in an inverted position, with the smallest bowl at the top. Inside the pit next to the skeleton's crossed wrists was a Walhalla Corrugated jar, and at her feet lay a Virgin Black-on-white canteen (see Fig. 33).

Besides these pots, burial 53 was accompanied by the most spectacular artifact found during any of the SAR excavations in Grand Canyon National Park. Around her right wrist was a bracelet made of 139 tiny beads of a shalelike material and 27 turquoise beads and pendants.

198

Much of the bracelet was still in place at the time of excavation (Fig. 57) and so could be reconstructed nearly to its original form.

FIG. 57. Detail of turquoise beads in situ around wrist of burial 53.

Appendix C

CHIPPED STONE ARTIFACTS

The taxonomy used to classify the chipped stone artifacts of the Walhalla Plateau is the same employed in an earlier study of material from Unkar Delta and discussed at length in Schwartz, Chapman, and Kepp (1980). The taxonomy is based on two underlying assumptions: first, that the manufactured form of an artifact is in some way related to its intended use, and second, that wear patterns on the artifact are indicative of its actual function. Given these assumptions, the taxonomy is designed to describe the chipped stone material in terms of attributes reflecting both manufacture and use. The analysis therefore focuses upon variability in overall artifact form, method of manufacture, and wear patterns.

The chipped stone collection was initially divided into five broad categories (Table 12) defined as follows:

Cores: pieces of parent material from which flakes have been detached;

Debitage: flakes that remained unmodified by either retouch or use subsequent to their detachment from cores;

Utilized flakes: flakes that were not modified by retouching but that exhibited wear patterns indicative of use;

Marginally retouched artifacts: flakes that had been retouched along one or more portions of their perimeters, the retouch flake

201

scars extending no more than one-third of the way across the flake's ventral or dorsal surface, or both;

Bifacially retouched artifacts: flakes that had been retouched along one or more portions of their perimeters so that the retouch flake scars extended more than one-third of the way across both the ventral and dorsal surfaces of the flake.

The bifacially retouched artifacts were classified in a fairly traditional manner, each artifact being placed in a single category chiefly on the basis of form. However, functionally descriptive type names were generally avoided because the actual functions of the tools were often uncertain. Instead, most of the type names of the bifacially modified artifacts describe formal attributes.

Marginally retouched artifacts were dealt with in a somewhat less customary way because many of them displayed two or more edges with different forms or wear patterns, indicating a great deal of multi-functionality. It was felt that these artifacts could not reasonably be assigned to a single taxonomic category, nor was it feasible to define additional categories to cover all combinations of tool forms or functions. To resolve this problem, the working edges of the artifacts were analyzed both individually and as combinations on whole implements. Each working edge was examined separately and assigned to a taxon on the basis of form or wear patterns.

All edges that could be formally characterized as projections were labeled "gouges" on the assumption that projections, as a distinct form, were used in some kind of gouging action. The remaining edges were divided into two groups on the basis of wear patterns documented by other researchers as being the results of certain uses. Edges exhibiting step fracture were classified as scrapers, and those displaying a form of wear known as attrition were called knives. (For a complete discussion of these wear patterns, see Schwartz, Chapman, and Kepp 1980.) Within each of these larger categories, subtypes were defined on the basis of attributes such as edge placement, edge shape, or additional wear patterns.

Before the artifacts are described, some of the terms used in the descriptions should be defined as they are used in this appendix.

Edge: any discrete portion of the perimeter of an artifact that exhibits a continuous wear pattern or characteristic formal attribute.

Edge outline: the shape of the edge as it appears when the artifact is placed flat and viewed from above; the five outlines recognized are straight, convex, concave, concave-convex, and projections.

Projections: any portions of a flake perimeter that meet in an acute angle, whether at a naturally occurring juncture or at a point manufactured on an otherwise straight or convex portion of the perimeter.

Sinuous edge: one that exhibits a series of projecting "teeth" produced by retouching such that the flake scars do not overlap but have prominent ridges between them; the range is from truly serrate to irregularly sinuous.

Smooth edge: a nonsinuous edge produced by retouching such that the flake scars do overlap regularly.

Retouching: any intentional modification of a flake subsequent to its detachment from a core.

Unidirectional retouch: pressure or percussion flaking of an edge on either its dorsal or ventral surface, but not on both; the term is also used in reference to the locations of wear patterns.

Bidirectional retouch: similar to the preceding except that retouch flakes have been removed from both the ventral and dorsal surfaces of the edge.

Edge angle: the angle between the ventral and dorsal surfaces of the edge itself, rather than that between the surfaces of the artifact on which the edge occurs.

CORES AND CORE TOOLS

Cores (Fig. 58)

Number: 121.
Size: maximum diameter of striking platform 3.0–8.0 cm (mean 4.8 cm); maximum length 1.7–8.0 cm (mean 3.5 cm).
Material: Kaibab chert (119), exotic chert (1), chalcedony (1).
Cores were defined as pieces of stone that exhibited two or more flake scars over 15 mm long on their surfaces but that had no bulbs of

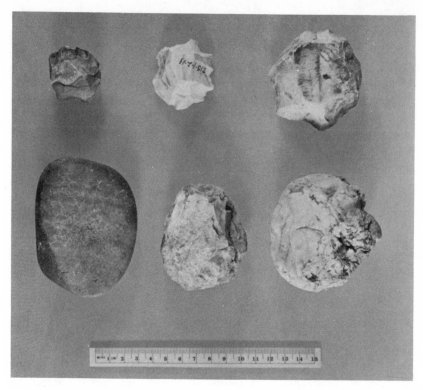

FIG. 58. Cores (top row), hammerstones (bottom row).

percussion. Most cores recovered from the Walhalla Glades were remnants of nodules of Kaibab chert. They varied considerably in size but were quite similar in form.

To prepare a chert nodule for knapping, it was first split to expose its interior structure. Less frequently, a large flake was detached from the nodule, and if the chert appeared fine enough in structure for the production of tools, the flat surface or facet created in the first step was then used as a striking platform for detaching flakes. The cortex was generally removed from most of the surface of the nodule, and much of the debitage in the Walhalla Glades collection consisted of these cortical flakes. Usually a single striking platform served for the detachment of nearly all flakes from a core, though occasionally flakes were removed from new surfaces created by previous flake detachment from the primary striking platform. There was no clear evidence that any technique other than hard-hammer percussion was used in the knapping process.

The recovered cores, which presumably had been discarded after they became too small for further flaking, were generally conical in shape, the primary striking platform being the base of the cone. The maximum dimension of the striking platform usually exceeded the length or thickness of the core. A few cores had been prepared through bidirectional flaking of a single edge from which other flakes were then detached alternately from each side.

Hammerstones* (Fig. 58)

Number: 13.
Size: length 5.8–10.2 cm (mean 7.2 cm); width 3.3–8.2 cm (mean 5.7 cm); thickness 2.9–5.7 cm (mean 4.3 cm).
Material: predominately chert, some quartzite.
Hammerstones were core tools showing evidence of use as hammers. Most of them had been reduced from their original sizes by the removal of flakes, though some, particularly those made from quartzite cobbles, retained most or all of the natural cortex. All specimens were characterized by battering scars. On spherical specimens, these scars generally occurred over much of the surface, but on those with cylindrical and oval shapes, the scars were usually limited to the ends of the stones.

Although a few hammerstones may initially have been manufactured or used as hammers—this is especially true of some of the quartzite cobbles—many specimens appeared to have first been used for the manufacture of flakes and later as hammers when they reached a size that could be held comfortably in the hand. Hammerstones were probably used in manufacturing chipped stone implements by hard-hammer flaking, as pecking stones to shape ground stone implements and pieces of stone masonry, and perhaps in other, less obvious ways.

Choppers

Number: 12.
Size: length 6.3–10.7 cm (mean 8.0 cm); width 2.5–9.1 cm (mean 6.3 cm); thickness 1.9–5.5 cm (mean 3.5 cm).

---

*The descriptions of hammerstones and choppers were written by Theodore R. Reinhart.

Material: chert.

Choppers were relatively large core tools that had at least one cutting edge. They were irregular in shape, showing little or no modification beyond that of the working edge. Any additional modification apparently served to reduce the core to a size that could conveniently be held in the hand. Except on the working edge and on any reduced portions, the cortex was left intact. The working edge was produced by the removal of flakes by either the hard- or the soft-hammer technique. Generally, choppers were worked only unifacially, but some specimens were bifacially flaked, and those implements had somewhat sinuous edges.

BIFACIALLY RETOUCHED ARTIFACTS

The bifacially retouched artifacts from the Walhalla Glades numbered 291. They were classified into 20 types according to criteria of thickness, overall form, and presence or position of notches. The two primary categories were thinned bifaces, or those measuring 8.0 mm or less in thickness, and unthinned bifaces, which had thicknesses of more than 8.0 mm.

Small Thinned Bifaces: Projectile Points (Fig. 59)

Among the smaller of the thinned bifaces were 103 specimens that warranted the functional designation of projectile points. All of these were triangular in shape and were produced by pressure retouching. The pressure flakes were oriented in varying directions but were chiefly perpendicular to the modified edge. In most specimens, the flake scars extended consistently to the midline of the point.

Unnotched Points
Number: 46 (24 whole, 22 fragmentary).
Size: length 18–54 mm (mean 28 mm); width 7–19 mm (mean 15 mm); thickness 2–6 mm (mean 3 mm).
Material: Kaibab chert (25), exotic chert (10), exotic chalcedony (9), obsidian (2).
Base form: straight to slightly concave (33), markedly concave (12), no data (1).

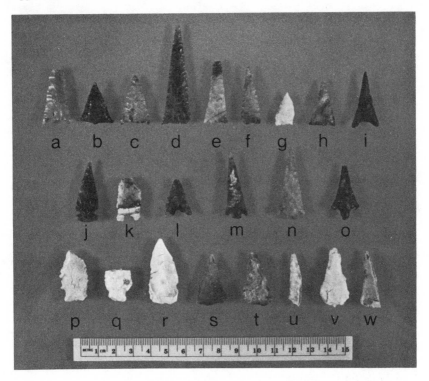

FIG. 59. Projectile points and drills. a–i: unnotched; j: side-notched; k: basally notched; l: side- and basally notched; m–o: corner-notched; p,q: miscellaneous; r–t: blanks; u–w: drills.

Edge form: straight, smooth (40), straight, sinuous (4), slightly concave, smooth (2).

Wear: attrition on lateral edges (22), no wear (17), drill wear (4); distal ends often showed polish.

Corner-Notched Points

Number: 23 (14 whole, 9 fragmentary).

Size: length 20–40 mm (mean 28 mm); width 10–20 mm (mean 14 mm); thickness 2–5 mm (mean 3.5 mm).

Material: Kaibab chert (10), exotic chert (7), exotic chalcedony (4), obsidian (2).

Base form: the corner notching produced a rather pronounced, straight-sided tang in 4 specimens and a short tang in 9. The remainder were broken. Nearly all specimens exhibited well-defined barbs.

Edge form: smooth (21), slightly sinuous (2).

Wear: attrition on lateral edges (16), no wear (7). The distal edges were often polished.

Basally-Notched Points

Number: 1 (fragmentary).

Size: width 14 mm, thickness 4 mm.

Material: exotic chert.

Base form: a single notch in the center of the base was 3 mm deep and produced barbs on either side.

Edge form: straight; serrations begin 6 mm above base.

Wear: attrition on lateral edges.

Side-Notched Points

Number: 2 (whole).

Size: length 31 mm, width 11 mm, thickness 3 mm; length 34 mm, width 13 mm, thickness 4 mm.

Material: exotic chert (1), obsidian (1).

Notches: situated 3–4 mm above the base.

Base form: slightly convex (1), slightly concave (1).

Edge form: straight to slightly convex, smooth.

Wear: attrition on lateral edges; one specimen used as a drill.

Side-Notched and Basally-Notched Points

Number: 1 (Whole).

Size: length 22 mm, width 16 mm, thickness 4 mm.

Material: chalcedony.

Notches: this specimen had a single notch in the center of its base and a notch in each lower lateral edge. This modification produced roughly triangular corner tangs at the proximal end of the point, the tangs being attached to the body of the point by a constricted neck.

Edge form: straight to slightly convex, somewhat sinuous.

Wear: none.

Miscellaneous Points

Number: 2 (1 whole, 1 fragmentary).

Size: length 24 (1 specimen), width 16 mm (both), thickness 5 mm (both).

Material: Kaibab chert (1), exotic chert (1).

Edge form: slightly convex; one serrate edge on the whole specimen, all other edges smooth.

Wear: polish on distal end (1).

These specimens, both found at site WP5, were classified as miscellaneous because they could not adequately be described by any of the formal categories used here. The specimen that was complete exhibited a slightly concave base, and though it was not actually notched, it did constrict slightly above the base to produce a short tang flaring slightly outward. The fragmentary specimen exhibited a very definite, wide tang formed on one side by a small side notch and on the other by what might have been a corner notch.

Projectile Point Blanks

Number: 21 (16 whole, 5 fragmentary).

Size: length 16–40 mm (mean 28 mm); width 10–23 mm (mean 16 mm); thickness 3–7 mm (mean 5 mm).

Material: exotic chert (9), Kaibab chert (8), exotic chalcedony (2), obsidian (2).

All these specimens seemed to represent various stages in the manufacture of projectile points. Eight of them exhibited modification over all of both surfaces, done mainly by percussion flaking. The remainder showed pressure flaking along their edges but not necessarily over their entire surfaces. The blanks apparently had not been finished because of breakage, extreme curvature of the flake, or other, undetermined reasons.

Projectile Point Fragments

Number: 7.

Size: width 9–15 mm (mean 12 mm); thickness 2–5 mm (mean 4 mm).

Material: chalcedony (3), Kaibab chert (1), obsidian (2), exotic chert (1).

These specimens were included in the projectile point category on the basis of their width and thickness. They included 6 distal portions and 2 midsections.

Small Thinned Bifaces: Drills (Fig. 59)

Number: 4 (all whole).

Size: length 24–33 mm (mean 29 mm); width 7–17 mm (mean 11 mm); thickness 3–6 (mean 4.5 mm).

Material: Kaibab chert (3), exotic chert (1).

These specimens were classified as drills because they exhibited step fracture indicative of rotary usage on their distal ends. One specimen was completely modified bifacially, and its lateral edges constricted about 18 mm above the convex base to form a shaft 15 mm long and 9 mm in diameter. The other specimens exhibited no basal modification but were retouched along the edges. The utilized portions of their shafts ranged from 8 mm to 25 mm long and from 5 mm to 8 mm in diameter. All the shafts were ovate in cross section.

Large Thinned Bifaces (Fig. 60)

The larger of the thinned bifaces included 124 specimens that were divided into five main types using criteria of basal modification (notching) and, in one case, edge modification in the form of "backing" or blunting of the edge. All of these specimens were triangular in shape, resembling the projectile points but somewhat larger in size. The retouch flakes taken from the large thinned bifaces were generally oriented perpendicular to the modified edge and extended consistently to the midline of the artifact.

Unnotched Large Thinned Bifaces
Number: 33 (10 whole, 23 fragmentary).
Size: length 39–99 mm (mean 52 mm); width 17–36 mm (mean 24 mm); thickness 4–8 mm (mean 6 mm).
Material: Kaibab chert (18), exotic chert (13), exotic chalcedony (2).
Base form: convex (21), straight (11), slightly concave with a small, flaring barb on at least one side (1).
Edge form: all straight or slightly convex; most irregularly sinuous but none truly serrate.
Wear: attrition on one or both lateral edges (24), no wear (6), attrition and step fracture on lateral edges (2), polish (1).

At least 18 of these specimens were manufactured by pressure retouching, the others primarily by soft-hammer percussion. Many of the latter may be unfinished blanks.

Corner-Notched Large Thinned Bifaces
Number: 7 (3 whole, 4 fragmentary).
Size: length 33–39 mm (mean 35 mm); width 18–25 mm (mean 22 mm); thickness 4–5 mm (mean 4 mm).

210

FIG. 60. Large thinned bifaces. a: side-notched; b: basally notched; c–e: corner-notched; f–m: unnotched; n–p: backed knives.

Material: exotic chert (5), Kaibab chert (1), chalcedony (1).

Base form: five specimens were clearly corner notched; the remaining two exhibited more variability in the placement of their notches. All exhibited definite tangs that flared outward at the base to varying degrees. Six specimens had barbs, a few of which flared outward slightly.

Edge form: straight (4), convex (1), indeterminable (2); serrate or irregularly sinuous (3), smooth (2), one edge serrate and one smooth (2).

Wear: attrition on one or both lateral edges (5), polish on both edges (1), indeterminable (1).

Side-Notched Large Thinned Bifaces

Number: 6 (3 whole, 3 fragmentary).

Size: length 42–44 mm (mean 43 mm); width 17–31 mm (mean 23 mm); thickness 5–6 mm (mean 5 mm).

Material: Kaibab chert (4), exotic chert (2).

Notches: five of these specimens exhibited true side notches; the sixth had one side and one corner notch but was arbitrarily included in this category. The last specimen was the only one that exhibited a barb, which occurred on its corner-notched side. Nearly all notches were placed between 4 and 5 mm above the bases of the artifacts.

Base form: straight (3), slightly concave (2), convex (1).

Edge form: straight (4), slightly convex (2); smooth (5), irregularly sinuous (1).

Wear: all exhibited attrition on at least one lateral edge, and one also showed step fracture and polish on its distal end.

Basally-Notched Large Thinned Bifaces

Number: 1 (whole).

Size: length 33 mm, width 23 mm, thickness 5 mm.

Material: exotic chert.

Base form: the basal notches produced a straight-sided, 5-mm-long tang with barbs on either side.

Edge form: slightly convex; smooth to somewhat sinuous.

Wear: none.

Backed Knives

Number: 9 (all whole).

Size: length 24–44 mm (mean 34 mm); width 12–26 mm (mean 19 mm); thickness 4–8 mm (mean 6 mm).

212

Material: Kaibab chert (6), exotic chert (2), exotic chalcedony (1).

Wear: all exhibited attrition on the utilized edge; one specimen had a retouched projection that had been used as a drill.

All these specimens were fragments of large thinned bifaces that either had broken accidentally or had been snapped deliberately, producing a flat surface or "backing" opposite the remaining lateral edge. All had been bifacially retouched prior to breakage, which, when deliberate, was usually accomplished by a blow to the face of the artifact and occasionally by striking the edge of the artifact.

Large Thinned Biface Fragments

Number: 68.

Size: width 11–34 mm (mean 21 mm); thickness 3–8 mm (mean 5 mm).

Material: exotic chert (46), Kaibab chert (21), chalcedony (1).

Wear: attrition was observed on most specimens, usually on one lateral edge; if on both, the attrition was generally more pronounced on one edge than on the other; occasional step fracture and polish.

Four of these specimens were fragments of large thinned bifaces that had been either side notched or corner notched. The basal tangs remained on two of these, while the other two were midsections from which the tangs had broken off. Another 27 were distal fragments classified as large thinned bifaces because of their width and thickness. Of these distal fragments, 15 had been shaped by percussion rather than by pressure flaking, and some may have been unfinished blanks. The remaining 37 fragments were midsections and other miscellaneous portions not exceeding 8 mm in thickness.

Unthinned Bifaces (Fig. 61)

The 60 unthinned bifaces were divided into six types on the basis of gross outline or the presence of backing. All specimens had been manufactured by soft-hammer percussion, which produced irregularly sinuous edges. Many specimens still exhibited remaining areas of cortex.

Triangular Outline

Number: 6 (1 whole, 5 fragmentary).

Size: length 50 mm (whole specimen); width 24–32 mm (mean 29 mm); thickness 10–17 mm (mean 12 mm).

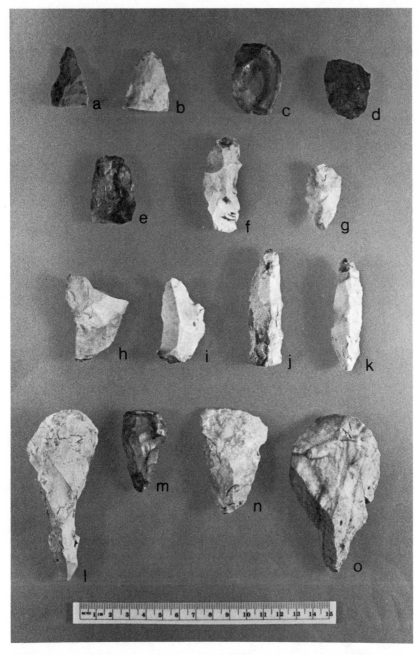

FIG. 61. Unthinned bifaces. a,b: triangular; c,d: ovate; e–g: rectangular; h,i: backed knives; j,k: cylinders; l–o: wide-bladed with constricting shaft.

Material: Kaibab chert (4), exotic chert (2).

Form: pointed distal ends and straight to convex lateral edges.

Wear: variable, ranging from considerable attrition on both lateral edges to step fracture and heavy polish. This variability suggests that the artifacts were not functionally uniform even though they were morphologically similar.

Rectangular Outline

Number: 11 (all whole).

Size: length 39–58 mm (mean 48 mm); width 16–28 mm (mean 23 mm); thickness 9–16 mm (mean 12 mm).

Material: Kaibab chert (9), exotic chert (2).

Wear: attrition or step fracture on small portions of the edges (9); no wear (2).

All these specimens had been retouched to a roughly rectangular shape by soft-hammer percussion, but in 8 cases portions of the cortex had not been removed. The artifacts also had very low ratios of width to thickness. For these reasons, many were thought to be unfinished blanks.

Ovate Outline

Number: 6 (all whole).

Size: length 34–47 mm (mean 41 mm); width 28–44 mm (mean 34 mm); thickness 12–18 mm (mean 14 mm).

Material: Kaibab chert (5), exotic chert (1).

Wear: attrition or step fracture over small portions of the edges (2), no wear (2).

Five of these specimens exhibited small areas of unremoved cortex, and this class, like the preceding category, was thought to represent the initial stage of manufacture of some other kind of implement.

Backed Knives

Number: 9 (all whole).

Size: length 27–71 mm (mean 49 mm); width 17–39 mm (mean 26 mm); thickness 8–16 mm (mean 12 mm).

Material: exotic chert (5), Kaibab chert (4).

Wear: all exhibited attrition along the edge opposite the backing; one specimen also had a utilized projection at one end.

Only two of these specimens had originally been manufactured as backed knives, the backing being formed by the removal of a few flakes from one side. Six other specimens had once been part of larger implements but had been remodified to produce a flat surface opposite one lateral edge. The ninth specimen was produced by crushing one of the retouched lateral edges to blunt it. Nearly all the cortex had been removed from these artifacts.

Wide-Bladed Unthinned Bifaces with Constricting Shafts

Number: 13 (12 whole, 1 fragmentary).

Size: length 48–111 mm (mean 65 mm); width 24–56 mm (mean 37 mm); thickness 8–24 mm (mean 15 mm).

Material: Kaibab chert (12), exotic chert (1).

Edge form: lateral edges convex (6), straight (5), concave (1), no data (1); distal edges all convex.

Distal edge angle: 37–83 degrees (mean 64 degrees).

Wear: polish or polish and slight attrition on distal edge (10), no wear (3); one specimen also had striations running at a 60 degree angle from the distal edge.

These specimens were all nearly triangular in shape with constricted proximal ends and distal ends that had been retouched to form rather wide edges or blades. Nine specimens were bifacially retouched on both ends by soft-hammer percussion, and the remainder were shaped by varying combinations of bifacial, unifacial, and marginal retouch. Ten specimens had been retouched on at least one side to increase the constriction of the proximal end.

Cylinders

Number: 6 (5 whole, 1 fragmentary).

Size: length 56–76 mm (mean 67 mm); width 17–23 mm (mean 20 mm); thickness 15–21 mm (mean 18 mm).

Material: Kaibab chert (6).

These specimens were essentially cylindrical in shape and had been manufactured by bifacial soft-hammer percussion and crushing. In cross section they approached a circular shape, though most of them exhibited at least three lengthwise ridges formed by the intersection of the "sides" from which flakes were removed. These ridges had been extensively battered and crushed, presumably to facilitate the holding of the implement in the hand. All but one specimen exhibited grinding wear or severe abrasion on at least one end, the wear often being limited to discrete portions of the end.

The function of these artifacts remains unknown. Schroeder (1955) reported two such implements from Zion National Park, Utah, where

216

they were found in a leather bag along with iron pyrite spheres and feathers, suggesting that they served as part of a strike-a-light kit. However, microscopic examination of the specimens from the Walhalla Glades revealed polish and other wear characteristics that argued against such a function. Furthermore, experimental use of one specimen as a retouching implement produced wear unlike that originally found on the artifact.

Unthinned Biface Fragments
Number: 9.
Size: width 23–42 mm (mean 33 mm); thickness 9–13 mm (mean 10 mm).
Material: Kaibab chert (9).

These specimens were all fragments of bifacially retouched artifacts measuring 9 mm or more in thickness. Three of them could be identified as midsections of straight-sided or convex-sided implements.

MARGINALLY RETOUCHED ARTIFACTS

Gouges

Of the marginally retouched artifacts, 415 specimens exhibited 483 gouge edges—that is, projections. They included 132 uniformal artifacts, those exhibiting one type of gouge projection only, which had a total of 137 such use edges. The remaining specimens were multiformal, displaying knife, scraper, or other kinds of gouge edges. Five types of gouges were distinguished in the Walhalla Glades lithic collection, four of them based on wear patterns and the fifth on form alone.

Rotary Gouges
Number: 80 artifacts, 83 edges; 35 of these uniformal (35 edges), 45 multiformal (48 edges).
Uniformal artifact size: length 21–57 mm (mean 34 mm); width 9–42 mm (mean 20 mm); thickness 2–20 mm (mean 9 mm).
Gouge projection size: length 1.1–13.3 mm (mean 4.8 mm); width 1.0–14.0 mm (mean 5.5 mm); thickness 0.7–9.7 mm (mean 3.4 mm).

These specimens were characterized by step fracture or, less commonly, striations on the projection shaft, indicating use in a rotary or drill-like fashion. Many projections also exhibited polish. The projections were predominately oval to circular in cross section as a result both of use and of retouching of the shaft.

Perforator Gouges

Number: 68 artifacts, 73 edges; 21 of these uniformal (22 edges), 47 multiformal (51 edges).

Uniformal artifact size: length 18–42 mm (mean 27 mm); width 10–30 mm (mean 18 mm); thickness 4–14 mm (mean 7 mm).

Gouge projection size: length 1.0–7.0 mm (mean 2.9 mm); width 1.2–8.8 mm (mean 3.2 mm); thickness 0.8–5.3 mm (mean 2.0 mm).

This type includes all projections other than square-tipped gouges that exhibited wear in the form of polish only. The polish extended evenly over the sides and ends of the projection shafts and presumably indicates use in perforating fairly soft materials. Most of the projection shafts were oval to circular in cross section.

Gouges with Unidirectional Wear

Number: 143 artifacts, 151 edges; 38 of these uniformal (40 edges), 105 multiformal (111 edges).

Uniformal artifact size: length 14–64 mm (mean 34 mm); width 10–38 mm (mean 22 mm); thickness 3–28 mm (mean 10 mm).

Gouge projection size: length 1.2–10.8 mm (mean 3.3 mm); width 1.9–12.5 mm (mean 4.7 mm); thickness 1.0–6.7 mm (mean 2.5 mm).

This type includes all projections other than square-tipped ones that exhibited unidirectional step fracture on their tips and occasionally on their shafts as well. Many specimens also displayed polish on the tip. Nearly all projections were plano-convex in cross section, and all were characterized by rounded or pointed tips. Presumably these gouges were used for incising fairly resistant materials.

Gouges with Bidirectional Wear (Fig. 62)

Number: 96 artifacts, 100 edges; 20 of these uniformal (20 edges), 76 multiformal (80 edges).

Uniformal artifact dimensions: length 20–69 mm (mean 33 mm); width 8–32 mm (mean 19 mm); thickness 4–18 mm (mean 8 mm).

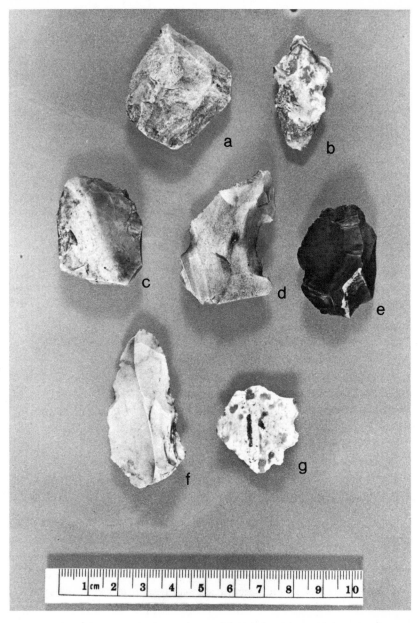

FIG. 62. Marginally retouched artifacts. a: square-tip gouge; b: gouge with bidirectional wear; c: convex sinuous side scraper; d: concave side scraper; e: convex sinuous end scraper; f: bidirectionally retouched sinuous knife; g: unidirectionally retouched sinuous knife.

Gouge projection size: length 1.1–7.0 mm (mean 3.0 mm); width 1.4–10.3 mm (mean 4.3 mm); thickness 0.9–6.0 mm (mean 2.4 mm).

This type includes all projections other than square-tipped gouges that exhibited either crushing of the tip or bidirectional step fracture perpendicular to the tip. Some exhibited slight polish as well. The projections ranged from plano-convex to oval or nearly circular in cross section, the plano-convex form predominating. The tips were rounded or pointed. The wear patterns on these specimens suggest that they were used to penetrate fairly resistant materials.

Square-Tipped Gouges (Fig. 62)
   Number: 73 artifacts, 76 edges; 18 of these uniformal (20 edges), 55 multiformal (56 edges).
   Uniformal artifact size: length 20–72 mm (mean 38 mm); width 13–29 mm (mean 20 mm); thickness 3–18 mm (mean 8 mm).
   Gouge projection size: length 1.4–7.0 mm (mean 3.6 mm); width 2.2–8.0 mm (mean 5.6 mm); thickness 0.6–5.1 mm (mean 2.5 mm).

These gouges were characterized by unidirectional retouching of the distal end of the projection shaft that produced a square tip. Nearly all projections were plano-convex in cross section. Most of the specimens exhibited unidirectional step fracture along the tip, while some displayed bidirectional step fracture, attrition, or polish.

Side Scrapers

This category of marginally retouched tools includes all straight, convex, or concave nonprojection working surfaces located on the lateral edges of flakes and exhibiting wear in the form of step fracture perpendicular to the long axis of the edge. A total of 433 such edges was identified, 121 of them occurring on 109 uniformal tools—that is, on flakes exhibiting only one kind of side scraper edge. The remaining 312 edges appeared on multiformal tools, those with knife, gouge, or other scraper edges. Five types were defined within this category on the basis of gross edge outline (straight, convex, or concave) and the sinuousness or smoothness of the edges.

Straight Sinuous Side Scrapers

Number: 64 artifacts, 71 edges; 18 of these uniformal (20 edges), 46 multiformal (51 edges).

Uniformal artifact size: length 31–60 mm (mean 40 mm); width 16–36 mm (mean 26 mm); thickness 5–19 mm (mean 11 mm).

Edge measurements: mean length 20.3 mm; mean edge angle 82 degrees.

This edge form was produced by unidirectional retouching done so that the detached flakes did not overlap, leaving prominent ridges between the flake scars. The edges were irregularly sinuous to almost serrate.

Straight Smooth Side Scrapers

Number: 134 artifacts, 142 edges; 43 of these uniformal (51 edges), 91 multiformal (91 edges).

Uniformal artifact size: length 16–72 mm (mean 35 mm); width 9–49 mm (mean 23 mm); thickness 3–20 mm (mean 9 mm).

Edge measurements: mean length 14.0 mm; mean edge angle 82 degrees.

This edge form was produced by unidirectional retouching done so that the detached flakes overlapped considerably, leaving no prominent ridges between the flake scars.

Convex Sinuous Side Scrapers (Fig. 62)

Number: 33 artifacts, 35 edges; 15 of these uniformal (16 edges), 18 multiformal (19 edges).

Uniformal artifact size: length 19–82 mm (mean 41 mm); width 12–40 mm (mean 28 mm); thickness 3–19 mm (mean 12 mm).

Edge measurements: mean length 23.6 mm; mean edge angle 79 degrees.

Some edges on these specimens were nearly serrate because of the even spacing of the nonoverlapping flake scars, but most were unevenly sinuous.

Convex Smooth Side Scrapers

Number: 67 artifacts, 68 edges; 18 of these uniformal (19 edges), 49 multiformal (49 edges).

Uniformal artifact size: length 24–49 mm (mean 37 mm); width 16–45 mm (mean 26 mm); thickness 5–17 mm (mean 10 mm).

221

Edge measurements: mean length 16.2 mm; mean edge angle 82 degrees.

Concave Side Scrapers (Fig. 62)
   Number: 106 artifacts, 117 edges; 15 of these uniformal (15 edges), 91 multiformal (102 edges).
   Uniformal artifact size: length 26–74 mm (mean 43 mm); width 12–53 mm (mean 26 mm); thickness 5–16 mm (mean 10 mm).
   Edge measurements: mean length 7.2 mm; mean edge angle 84 degrees.
   Some of these specimens had deliberately been manufactured by unidirectional retouch, often as part of the manufacture of gouge projections adjacent to the concave edges. Many, however, appeared to have been produced solely through use on rounded or cylindrical surfaces. Nearly all the edges were smooth rather than sinuous.

End Scrapers

End scrapers were defined according to the same criteria used for side scrapers, with one exception: the working edges were located on the ends, not the sides, of the flakes. The artifacts assigned to this category had 177 edges, 50 of them on uniformal specimens and 127 on multiformal ones. Within the category, five types were distinguished on the basis of edge outline and edge sinuousness or smoothness. Because the descriptions of end scrapers are identical to those of side scrapers, only measurements will be presented here.

Straight Sinuous End Scrapers
   Number: 22 artifacts, 22 edges; 8 of these uniformal (8 edges), 14 multiformal (14 edges).
   Uniformal artifact size: length 21–52 mm (mean 34 mm); width 12–34 mm (mean 23 mm); thickness 2–29 mm (mean 9 mm).
   Edge measurements: mean length 13.9 mm; mean edge angle 83 degrees.

Straight Smooth End Scrapers
   Number: 49 artifacts, 49 edges; 16 of these uniformal (16 edges), 33 multiformal (33 edges).

Uniformal artifact size: length 15–92 mm (mean 40 mm); width 11–50 mm (mean 25 mm); thickness 4–20 mm (mean 9 mm).

Edge measurements: mean length 12.3 mm; mean edge angle 85 degrees.

Convex Sinuous End Scrapers (Fig. 62)
Number: 23 artifacts, 23 edges; 6 of these uniformal (6 edges), 17 multiformal (17 edges).

Uniformal artifact size: length 23–53 mm (mean 35 mm); width 19–38 mm (mean 27 mm); thickness 6–15 mm (mean 10 mm).

Edge measurements: mean length 24.2 mm; mean edge angle 83 degrees.

Convex Smooth End Scrapers
Number: 49 artifacts, 50 edges; 16 of these uniformal (16 edges), 33 multiformal (34 edges).

Uniformal artifact size: length 21–48 mm (mean 33 mm); width 12–39 mm (mean 24 mm); thickness 5–18 mm (mean 10 mm).

Edge measurements: mean length 13.6; mean edge angle 84 degrees.

Concave End Scrapers
Number: 30 artifacts, 33 edges; 4 of these uniformal (4 edges), 26 multiformal (29 edges).

Uniformal artifact size: length 33–68 mm (mean 42 mm); width 21–32 mm (mean 26 mm); thickness 7–18 mm (mean 11 mm).

Edge measurements: mean length 6.7 mm; mean edge angle 87 degrees.

Concave-Convex Scrapers

Number: 44 artifacts, 45 edges; 12 of these uniformal (13 edges), 32 multiformal (32 edges).

Uniformal artifact size: length 25–81 mm (mean 44 mm); width 12–48 mm (mean 26 mm); thickness 3–21 mm (mean 21 mm).

Edge measurements: mean length 19.9 mm; mean edge angle 84 degrees.

These scrapers were defined as a separate category on the basis of (1) an undulating concave-convex edge outline produced by continuous unidirectional retouching and (2) unidirectional step fracture that was continuous along the entire working edge. All such edges were located on the sides of flakes and were smooth rather than sinuous. Most of the artifacts had one concave and one convex portion of each working edge, but a few exhibited two convex portions flanking a single concavity.

Knives

This category was established to include all nonprojection edges that exhibited attrition as a wear pattern. A total of 616 edges fit that criterion, occurring on 475 artifacts. Of these edges, 167 appeared on 154 uniformal specimens, and 449 edges occurred on the 417 multiformal tools. Five types were .established within the knife category on the basis of retouch modification and edge smoothness or sinuousness.

Unretouched Knives
   Number: 166 artifacts, 183 edges; 1 of these uniformal (1 edge), 165 multiformal (182 edges).
   Uniformal artifact size: length 49 mm, width 25 mm, thickness 12 mm.
   Edge measurements: mean length 21.3 mm; mean edge angle 49 degrees.
   Many of the marginally retouched artifacts in the collection exhibited one or more unretouched knife edges in addition to their retouched edges. These utilized knife edges are included here as a separate type, though they are undoubtedly underrepresented because utilized flakes as a category were not analyzed for wear patterns. These knife edges occurred primarily on the lateral edges of flakes.

Unidirectionally Retouched Sinuous Knives (Fig. 62)
   Number: 86 artifacts, 89 edges; 28 of these uniformal (29 edges), 58 multiformal (60 edges).
   Uniformal artifact size: length 28–77 mm (mean 41 mm); width 13–46 mm (mean 24 mm); thickness 3–23 mm (mean 9 mm).
   Edge measurements: mean length 22.3 mm; mean edge angle 60 degrees.
   These knife edges ranged in form from truly serrate, with fairly even spacing of the concavities and projections that formed the

224

teeth, to irregularly sinuous. The latter form predominated and exhibited attrition continuously along the working edge. Some serrate edges exhibited wear only on the projections of the teeth and not in the intervening concavities. Edge outlines were straight to slightly convex.

Unidirectionally Retouched Smooth Knives
    Number: 98 artifacts, 100 edges; 31 of these uniformal (32 edges), 67 multiformal (68 edges).
    Uniformal artifact size: length 15–61 mm (mean 38 mm); width 11–48 mm (mean 24 mm); thickness 3–25 mm (mean 8 mm).
    Edge measurements: mean length 21.5 mm; mean edge angle 59 degrees.
    These edges occurred primarily on the sides of flakes and were straight to slightly convex in outline.

Bidirectionally Retouched Sinuous Knives (Fig. 62)
    Number: 94 artifacts, 99 edges; 41 of these uniformal (42 edges), 53 multiformal (57 edges).
    Uniformal artifact size: length 20–76 mm (mean 38 mm); width 13–42 mm (mean 24 mm); thickness 4–21 mm (mean 9 mm).
    Edge measurements: mean length 23.7 mm; mean edge angle 61 degrees.
    The description of these artifacts is identical to that of unidirectionally retouched sinuous knives.

Bidirectionally Retouched Smooth Knives
    Number: 127 artifacts, 145 edges; 53 of these uniformal (63 edges), 74 multiformal (82 edges).
    Uniformal artifact size: length 15–56 mm (mean 34 mm); width 10–44 mm (mean 21 mm); thickness 3–19 mm (mean 8 mm).
    Edge measurements: mean length 20.5 mm; mean edge angle 61 degrees.
    These edges were predominately straight in outline and were usually located on the sides of flakes.

Appendix D

GROUND STONE ARTIFACTS

Ground stone artifacts were, as the name implies, formed by the grinding of their surfaces either as part of the manufacturing process or during use. Some of them served identifiable utilitarian purposes, examples being manos, metates, mortars, pestles, axes, and polishing stones. Others, mainly pendants and beads, were ornamental rather than utilitarian. Artifacts such as these, whose functions could be identified with some confidence, were assigned to categories with functionally descriptive names. Others that could not be so recognized were classified on the basis of form alone.

The ground stone artifacts recovered during the 1969 field season were studied by Theodore R. Reinhart, whose report constitutes most of this appendix. Jane Kepp edited and condensed the report for publication and classified the ground stone from sites GC378, GC408, and GC215, all excavated in 1970, according to Reinhart's typology. A few specimens in the 1970 material did not fit any of the earlier descriptions, so new categories were added to the typology to encompass them. A few comments on existing categories, based on Kepp's observations, are also included. In the following type descriptions, the size range is based on the entire collection; but unless noted otherwise, the mean is based only on the 1969 sample.

METATES

Number: 46.

Material: sandstone (33), limestone (13).

All whole or nearly whole metates from the Walhalla Glades were of the trough type (Fig. 63), their sides extending above the plane of the grinding surface. In most whole specimens, one end was also raised, the other end open. Two specimens had both ends open, and a third was of the type known as the Utah metate (Fig. 64). Of the 35 metate fragments recovered, 20 could be identified as trough metates and one as a slab metate. The remaining 14 were pieces of grinding surfaces whose forms were unrecognizable.

The initial shaping of a metate was accomplished by pecking the rock with a hammerstone. The working surface was formed primarily by use—the grinding action of a mano—but often the outside surfaces were also ground to produce regular sides, ends, and bottoms. Sometimes the working surface was pecked to roughen it when it became too smooth for effective grinding.

Sandstone and limestone from the Kaibab formation were used in manufacturing these implements. Kaibab limestone has a high sand content and, like sandstone, makes a suitable abrasive surface for grinding tools. The texture of the working surfaces of these metates was classified according to three relative and somewhat subjective grades: fine, medium, and coarse. This classification reflects both the grain of the raw material and the appearance of the working surface. Presumably the processing of maize involved breaking down the kernels on coarse-surfaced metates and then grinding them to increasingly finer consistencies on medium- and fine-grained implements.

Trough Metates Open at One End

Number: 8.

Material: sandstone (4), limestone (4).

Overall size: length 36–50 cm (mean 44 cm); width 25–36 cm (mean 32 cm); thickness 8–14 cm (mean 11 cm).

Trough size: length 31–44 cm (mean 39 cm); width 18–25 cm (mean 22 cm); depth 2–9 cm (mean 5 cm).

Surface texture: fine (1), medium (3), coarse (3), undetermined (1).

FIG. 63. Trough metates. (Scale is 16 cm long.)

FIG. 64. "Utah" trough metate. (Scale is 16 cm long.)

These rectangular metates had working surfaces bordered by raised sides and one raised end. The borders had rounded edges, and both faces were generally smoothed by grinding. The working surfaces sloped downward from the raised end to the open end, where the greatest depth of each trough was found.

One specimen from site GC378 was atypical in that it was unusually small, though quite thick, and had no definite raised border. However, the working surface that had been distinctly pecked out did not extend to the edges of the stone on three sides and apparently formed the initial stage of a trough metate open at one end.

Trough Metates Open at Both Ends

Number: 2 (1 whole, 1 fragmentary).

Material: sandstone.

Overall size (whole specimen): length 41 cm, width 35 cm, thickness 17 cm.

Trough size (whole specimen): length 41 cm, width 26 cm, depth 13 cm.

Surface texture: coarse (1), undetermined (1).

These artifacts were similar to the trough metates already described, except that both ends were open and the length of the grinding surface equaled the length of the implement. The working surfaces sloped from one end to the other. One open end was probably closed initially but through time had been worn away by extensive use.

230

Utah Trough Metate

Number: 1 (incomplete).
Material: limestone.
Overall size: width 30 cm, thickness 14 cm.
Trough size: width 19 cm, depth 8 cm.
Surface texture: coarse.

The Utah metate is of the trough type that is open only at one end, but it differs from other such implements in that a small platform lies adjacent to the working surface at the closed end. On this specimen, the grinding surface sloped from the platform toward the open end. The platform, which was bordered by a low rim on the sides and the closed end of the metate, measured 19 cm by 11 cm and showed no grinding wear. It was probably used to hold maize kernels or meal during the grinding operation.

Unclassified Trough Metates

Number: 20.
Material: sandstone (16), limestone (4).
Surface texture: fine (1), medium (4), coarse (14), undetermined (1).

These specimens were fragments of trough metates too incomplete for further classification.

Slab Metate

Number: 1.
Material: sandstone.
Surface texture: medium.

This fragment represented the only identifiable slab metate found in the Walhalla Glades. Its complete form and size could not be reconstructed, but the grinding surface sloped downward from the single edge present toward the broken portion, indicating that the piece could not have been the open end of a trough metate. The fragment was extremely worn, its minimum thickness being only 1.5 cm, and the undersurface was ground even smoother than the working surface.

Unclassified Metates

Number: 14.
Material: sandstone (10), limestone (4).
Surface texture: fine (3), medium (4), coarse (6), undetermined (1).
These metate fragments came mostly from grinding surfaces and were not diagnostic of the original form of the implements.

MANOS

Number: 150.
Material: sandstone (105), limestone (45).
Manos, the hand-held implements used in conjunction with metates, were generally rectangular stones with one or more grinding surfaces across the length of one or both faces (Fig. 65). All but 15 of the 150

FIG. 65. Manos. (Scale is 16 cm long.)

specimens recovered were classified into five types distinguished by their numbers of grinding surfaces and cross-sectional shapes. In many cases, these types probably represent different stages of wear that the manos had reached when they were discarded. The unclassified specimens included possible mano preforms and fragments too small to classify.

Like metates, manos were initially shaped by pecking, and their final form resulted from grinding wear. The texture of their working surfaces varied from fine to coarse, and again this gradation probably had functional significance. Only in one instance, at site GC212, was a mano recovered in direct association with a metate; both implements had coarse-textured surfaces.

Manos with One Grinding Surface and Rectangular Cross Section

Number: 38.

Material: sandstone (26), limestone (12).

Size: length 11–26 cm (mean 21 cm); width 8–12 cm (mean 10 cm); thickness 2–7 cm (mean 4 cm).

These manos were rectangular in both outline and cross section. Only one of the two faces of the implement had been used for grinding. The unused face was generally flat, either naturally so or as the result of pecking, while the ground face was flat or convex across its length. The edges were smooth and rounded, and the ends were also ground smooth, either from contact with the sides of the metate or through actual use. The sides of 18 specimens had grooves for finger holds—that is, long, narrow depressions about half the length of the mano itself, in the centers of both sides.

Manos with Two Opposed Grinding Surfaces

Number: 51.

Material: sandstone (46), limestone (5).

Size: length 8–24 cm (mean 20 cm); width 6.5–11 cm (mean 9 cm); thickness 3–5 cm (mean 4 cm).

This type of mano was similar to that just described, except that both faces were used in grinding. Again, different stages of wear were represented, and consequently some specimens diverged from the rectangular cross section of the idealized type. Depending on the ways in which the manos had been used, wear had produced rounded, faceted, or inclined surfaces rather than flat ones on some specimens. However, none of the manos assigned to this category had two distinct grinding surfaces on one face. Many manos of this type in the 1970 sample exhibited heavy wear on one face and much lighter grinding on the other. Side grooves were found on 8 specimens, and one had traces of red clay embedded in one face.

Manos with Two Grinding Surfaces on One Face

Number: 20.
Material: limestone (18), sandstone (2).
Size: length 13–24 cm (mean 19 cm); width 8–12 cm (mean 10 cm); width 2–4 cm (mean 2.5 cm).

These manos each had two grinding planes that met at an obtuse angle on one face, producing a quadrilateral cross section. The grinding surfaces were flat and the opposite face was generally the same; this face was sometimes pecked but not ground. The edges and corners were rounded, the sides and ends regular and, frequently, ground.

This mano form resulted apparently from the wearing down of one edge of the original grinding surface, which produced two distinct planes. If wear had continued, the surfaces would have become a single plane again, and the mano would have been triangular in cross section—a different formal type.

Manos with Three Grinding Surfaces

Number: 21.
Material: sandstone (17), limestone (4).
Size: length 14–21 cm (mean 19 cm); width 7–12 cm (mean 10 cm); thickness 3–1.5 cm (mean 2 cm).

This type of mano was identical to the preceding type, except that the flat face opposite the one with two grinding surfaces was also ground. This form probably represents a further stage of wear on manos that originally had two flat, opposed working surfaces.

234

Manos with One Grinding Surface and Triangular Cross Section

Number: 5.

Material: sandstone (3), limestone (2).

Size: length 18 cm (1 whole specimen); width 9–10 cm; thickness 2.8–3.3 cm.

These manos each had a single, slanted grinding surface on one face that gave the implement a triangular cross section. The other face was generally unworked and naturally flat. The sides and edges were regular, and the ends were ground.

Unclassified Manos

Number: 15.

Material: sandstone (11), limestone (4).

Four of the specimens in this category were rectangular stones that had been pecked into shape but showed no grinding wear. They probably were mano preforms, and their mean measurements were 18 cm in length, 11 cm in width, and 4 cm in thickness. The other 11 specimens were mano fragments too small to allow identification of their forms.

OTHER GRINDING IMPLEMENTS

Ground Slabs

Number: 2 (1 whole, 1 fragmentary).

Material: sandstone (2).

Size (whole specimen): length 18 cm, width 14 cm, thickness 1 cm.

These specimens from site GC215, both thin slabs of fine-grained sandstone, had obviously been used as surfaces upon which something was ground, but they could not formally be classed as metates. The fragmentary specimen had a single worked edge remaining that had been chipped and ground to form a straight side. Limited grinding wear could be seen on one face of the slab. The whole specimen had been ground smooth on all edges but was not regularly shaped. The central portion of one face exhibited grinding wear and striations.

Mortars (Fig. 66)

Number: 5.
Material: limestone (3), sandstone (2).
Size (all specimens): length 13–22 cm (mean 16 cm); width 12–15 cm (mean 14 cm); thickness 5–9 cm (mean 7 cm); depression diameter 7–11 cm (mean 9 cm); depression depth 2–4 cm (mean 3 cm).

Mortars were round or oblong stones with flat bottoms and circular, basin-shaped depressions in their upper surfaces. These depressions were initially formed by pecking and were further deepened by the pounding and grinding action of a hand-held pestle. The sides and bottom of the mortar were usually crudely formed or unworked, but in some cases the corners were rounded and the sides and bottom smoothed.

Pestles (Fig. 66)

Number: 2.
Material: sandstone (1), limestone (1).
Size: length 9–11 cm; width 6 cm; thickness 5–6 cm.
These specimens were cylinder-shaped implements with convex ends

FIG. 66. Mortars and pestles. (Scale is 16 cm long.)

236

that exhibited grinding and pounding wear. Their faces had been rounded and smoothed by pecking and grinding prior to use and by wear from the hands of the users. The ends were probably shaped primarily through use. The form of these tools and the extensive abrasion on their ends suggested that they served as hand-held pestles used in conjunction with mortars.

Sharpening Stones

Number: 2.
Material: sandstone (1), limestone (1).
Size: length 10–15 cm; width 5–13 cm; thickness 3.7–4.4 cm.

These rectangular slabs showed little or no modification except for grinding wear on one naturally flat or concave face that served as a sharpening and grinding surface. Striations were visible on these surfaces, generally paralleling the long axes of the implements and suggesting that the slabs were used for sharpening and grinding a variety of materials such as soft stone, wood, bone, and antler.

Atypical Grinding Stones (Fig. 67)

Three grinding implements found at site GC215 were unusual specimens not readily classifiable as manos. One piece made from fine-grained sandstone resembled a mano but was extremely small: 5 cm long, 4 cm wide, and 2 cm thick. It had been pecked and ground on all edges to a rectangular shape, and it was ground smooth on both faces. Such "miniature manos" were probably used on thin ground slabs rather than on metates.

The second specimen was a conical quartzite cobble with truncated, flat ends that had been used for both grinding and pounding. A small, battered depression on one face indicated that the specimen had also served as an anvil. It measured 10 cm long, 5–7 cm wide, and 3–6 cm thick.

The third atypical tool was a quartzite pebble that had been roughened by pecking over its entire surface and then used as a grinding tool. One face and side were ground fairly smooth, and the rougher face exhibited numerous striations. The specimen measured 13 cm long, 9.5 cm wide, and 4 cm thick.

FIG. 67. Square stones (a,b), atypical grinding stones (c–e). (Scale is 16 cm long.)

OTHER GROUND STONE ARTIFACTS

Axes (Fig. 68)

Number: 12 (11 whole, 1 fragmentary).
Material: quartzite (5), igneous rock (basalt?) (7).
Size (all whole specimens): length 8–22 cm (mean 5 cm); width 4–10 cm (mean 7 cm); thickness 1–7 cm (mean 5 cm).

Axes were among the more beautifully made stone tools found on the Walhalla Plateau. Eleven of the specimens were ground completely smooth and had sharp, polished blades and full grooves for hafting. A pronounced lip bordered each groove. Only the single fragmentary specimen had not been completely ground after being shaped by chipping. Four of the five axes from site GC215 were found together as a cache in the fill of a room (Fig. 69).

238

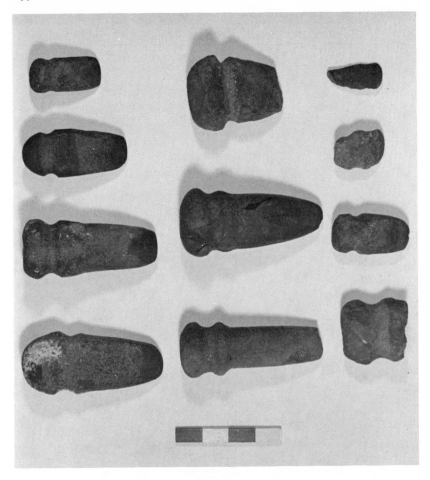

FIG. 68. Axes. The four axes cached at site GC215 are on the left. (Scale is 16 cm long.)

Pot Lids (Fig. 70)

Number: 5.
Material: sandstone (4), limestone (1).
Size (all specimens): diameter 7.5–19 cm (mean 15 cm); thickness 1–2 cm.

Pot lids, so called because they presumably were used to cover pots, were thin slabs whose edges had been chipped and ground to shapes

239

FIG. 69. Cache of stone axes found in room 7 at GC215.

FIG. 70. Pot lids (top row and lower left), shaped slab (lower right). (Scale is 16 cm long.)

240

ranging from circular to roughly rectangular with rounded corners. Except on specimens having naturally flat faces, the surfaces were also shaped by grinding. No i e wear was evident on any of the specimens.

Polishing Stones (Fig. 71)

Number: 17.
Material: quartzite (13), igneous rock (4).
Size: length 3–13 cm (mean 7 cm); width 3–12 cm (mean 5 cm); thickness 1–6 cm (mean 2.5 cm).

Polishing stones were pebbles of a variety of shapes and sizes that were unmodified except for polish and, sometimes, striations on one or more faces. These working surfaces were naturally smooth and flat and were not modified prior to utilization. Such pebbles were probably used to smooth and polish the surfaces of pottery vessels and, in the case of the larger specimens, possibly wall plaster and floor surfaces. The three specimens from sites GC378 and GC408 still had red clay embedded in their surfaces as well as evidence of light hammering wear on their sides or ends.

Square Stones (Fig. 67)

The two specimens of this type, both sandstone and both found in rooms at site GC212, were remarkably similar. They were slightly rectangular in outline and about half as thick as they were long, all faces having been smoothed by grinding, the corners and edges slightly rounded. The working surfaces were limited to small, rough depressions in the center of each face and most sides. These depressions, each about 10 mm in diameter and a few millimeters deep, appeared to have resulted from the pounding of some narrow, cylindrical or pointed object. Possibly the implements served as bases for other tools with wooden shafts, such as spindles.

Cylindrical Stones (Fig. 71)

Number: 7.
Material: basalt (7).

FIG. 71. Mudstone discs (top row), cylindrical stones (middle row), polishing stones (bottom row).

Size: length 8–9 cm; diameter 2–3.5 cm.

These specimens, all manufactured from vesicular basalt, were cylinder shaped with tapering convex ends. They had been shaped by grinding and were generally regular in form except for some unevenness caused by the coarse material. Two specimens exhibited grinding over one end that might have been caused by use, while the others showed no use wear. Four specimens were found in proximity to one another in room 12 at site GC212. The function of these artifacts is unknown.

Stone Ball

This specimen was a spherical piece of limestone 7 cm in diameter, the surface of which had been smoothed and polished by grinding. Its function is not known.

Flat Discs and Squares (Figs. 71 and 72)

Number: 16.

Material: mudstone (8), sandstone (8).

These artifacts were thin, flat pieces of stone that had been ground into the shapes of discs and squares with rounded corners. Both faces and all edges of each stone had been smoothed, possibly after some cutting or chipping to make the preform.

The eight mudstone specimens included five discs and one square, through the centers of which circular holes had been drilled. The discs with holes measured 4–6 cm in diameter and 3 mm thick, while the square was 4.3 cm by 4.5 cm by 5 mm thick. The eighth specimen was a disc without a drilled hole that measured 4 cm in diameter and 6 mm thick.

All the sandstone specimens were squares in which no holes had been drilled. They were considerably larger than the mudstone artifacts, averaging 11 cm long, 9 cm wide, and 1 cm thick.

It is possible that the circular specimens with holes functioned as spindle whorls, but in general the use of these artifacts is unknown. The larger sandstone squares probably served a different purpose from that of the mudstone specimens.

FIG. 72. Flat squares without holes.

Shaped Slabs (Fig. 70)

Number: 8.
Material: sandstone (8).

All these artifacts were fragments of thin, rectangular, sandstone slabs whose edges had been shaped by chipping and varying degrees of grinding. The recorded specimens all came from site GC215, but others not included in the ground stone analysis were recovered during the 1969 excavations. At least two slabs had once been quite large, although their remaining portions did not allow the original measurements to be reconstructed. These two slabs were found in rooms in positions suggesting that one had served as a doorway cover and the other as a roof entry cover. Other pieces may have been fragments of similar entrance covers, while at least one smaller specimen probably served a different, though unknown, purpose. None of the slabs exhibited any evidence of wear on the flat surfaces.

Beads (Fig. 73)

Number: 144.
Material: shale or pipestone (139), turquoise (4), crinoid fossil (1).

All but one of the ground stone beads found in the Walhalla Glades were part of a single bracelet found with burial 53 at GC212A. Of these, 139 were tiny specimens only 2 mm in both length and diameter and made of a soft, red, sedimentary rock, probably shale or pipestone. Four turquoise beads also appeared with this bracelet; they measured 4–6 mm in diameter and 1–4 mm long. The additional bead was a crinoid fossil with a hole in its center and some evidence of grinding around its edges.

Pendants (Fig. 73)

Pendants included 25 small pieces of stone ground to rectangular or square shapes, each having a drilled hole at the center of one end. A single atypical specimen was triangular and had two small grooves across one corner that were probably used for stringing the ornament. Twenty-three turquoise pendants were part of the bracelet found with

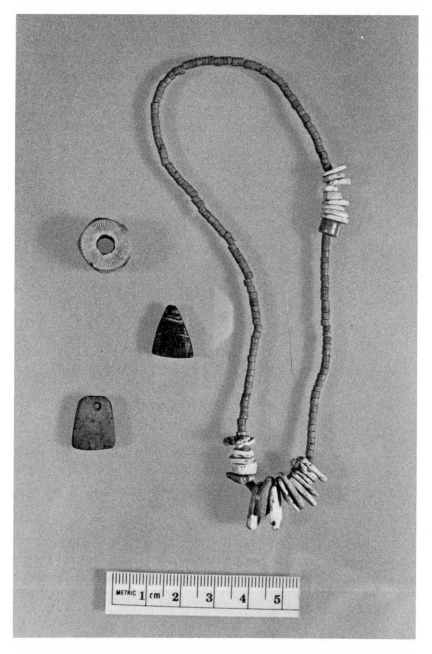

FIG. 73. Beads and pendants. Bracelet is from burial 53 at site GC212A.

burial 53 at GC212A. This turquoise was of poor quality and ranged in color from light green to light blue to almost white. The other two specimens were made of sandstone and soapstone.

Other Ornaments

Number: 3.
Material: soapstone (2), turquoise (1).
Size: length 14–35 mm (mean 24 mm); width 7–30 mm (mean 17 mm); thickness 3–9 mm (mean 5 mm).

This category included a large, irregular piece of soapstone and two smaller, rectangular pieces, one of soapstone and one of turquoise, with rounded sides and corners. All were flat and exhibited grinding wear on their surfaces, which were coarse on the soapstone specimens but smooth and polished on the turquoise specimen. All lacked holes for stringing. The large, irregular specimen was possibly a piece of raw material, and the smaller soapstone specimen might have been a preform for a pendant. The turquoise specimen, from burial 53 at GC212A, probably was a finished piece that was not intended for stringing.

Unidentifiable Ground Stone Fragments

This group included 41 pieces of sandstone and limestone that exhibited grinding wear but were too small to be identified by type.

MISCELLANEOUS STONE

Miscellaneous stone artifacts included unmodified concretions and minerals found in an archaeological context. Many such pebbles and concretions were not counted as artifacts because such pieces from the Kaibab limestone were common in natural contexts as well. Three concretions, however, had shapes that could be construed as anthropomorphic or zoomorphic, and these were possibly used as fetishes. Minerals such as hematite, yellow ochre, and turquoise did not occur naturally at the sites, and their presence was evidence of cultural use.

Four pieces of hematite and a single specimen of yellow ochre were found and were probably sources of paint pigments. Two pieces of unworked turquoise might have been raw material for ornaments or might have been used for ceremonial purposes.

The final miscellaneous stone artifact was a large, conical piece of limestone measuring 18 cm by 17 cm at its base and 14 cm high. The stone had apparently been shaped at least partially by pecking and scraping, but its original surface was somewhat eroded and its function could not be determined.

References

AUERBACH, HERBERT S.
1943 "Father Escalante's Journal, with Related Documents and Maps," *Utah Historical Quarterly,* vol. 11, no. 1–4 (Salt Lake City).

BRETERNITZ, DAVID A.
1966 *An Appraisal of Tree-Ring Dated Pottery in the Southwest,* Anthropological Papers of the University of Arizona, no. 10 (Tucson: University of Arizona Press).

BROWN, J. WILLIAM
1969 "Stratigraphy and Petrology of the Kaibab Formation Between Desert View and Cameron, Northern Arizona," in *Geology and Natural History of the Four Corners Region,* Four Corners Geological Society, Fifth Field Conference.

COLTON, HAROLD S.
1952 *Pottery Types of the Arizona Strip and Adjacent Areas in Utah and Nevada,* Museum of Northern Arizona Ceramic Series, no. 1 (Flagstaff).

1955 *Pottery Types of the Southwest,* Museum of Northern Arizona Ceramic Series, no. 3 (Flagstaff).

1956 *Pottery Types of the Southwest,* Museum of Northern Arizona Ceramic Series, no. 3C (Flagstaff).

1958 *Pottery Types of the Southwest,* Museum of Northern Arizona Ceramic Series, no. 3D (Flagstaff).

CUTLER, HUGH C., AND LEONARD W. BLAKE
1980   "Plant Materials from Grand Canyon Sites," Appendix B in *Archaeology of the Grand Canyon: Unkar Delta,* by D. W. Schwartz, R. C. Chapman, and J. Kepp, Grand Canyon Archaeological Series, vol. 2 (Santa Fe: School of American Research Press).

DEAN, JEFFREY S., AND WILLIAM J. ROBINSON
1977   *Dendroclimatic Variability in the American Southwest, A.D. 680 to 1970,* Laboratory of Tree-Ring Research, University of Arizona, Tucson, report to the National Park Service.

HALL, EDWARD T., JR.
1942   *Archaeological Survey of Walhalla Glades,* Museum of Northern Arizona Bulletin no. 20 (Flagstaff).

HAURY, EMIL W.
1931   *Kivas of the Tusayan Ruin, Grand Canyon, Arizona,* Medallion Papers, no. 9 (Gila Pueblo).

HOFFMEISTER, DONALD F.
1971   *Mammals of Grand Canyon* (Urbana: University of Illinois Press).

JAMES, GEORGE WHARTON
1900   *In and Around the Grand Canyon* (Boston: Little, Brown).

JUDD, NEIL M.
1926   *Archeological Observations North of the Rio Colorado,* Bureau of American Ethnology Bulletin no. 82 (Washington, D.C.).

MARSHALL, MICHAEL P.
1979   "Descriptions of New Ceramic Wares and Types," Appendix D in *Archaeology of the Grand Canyon: The Bright Angel Site,* by D. W. Schwartz, M. P. Marshall, and J. Kepp, Grand Canyon Archaeological Series, vol. 1 (Santa Fe: School of American Research Press).

MERKLE, JOHN
1962   "Plant Communities of the Grand Canyon Area, Arizona," *Ecology* 43:698–711.

RASMUSSEN, D. IRVIN
1941   "Biotic Communities of Kaibab Plateau, Arizona," *Ecological Monographs* 11:229–75.

REED, ERIK K.
1949   "The Significance of Skull Deformation in the Southwest," *El Palacio* 56: 100–119.

References

REINHART, THEODORE R.
1969 "Grand Canyon II Lithics," unpublished report on file at the School of American Research, Santa Fe.

SCHROEDER, ALBERT H.
1955 *Archaeology of Zion Park,* University of Utah Anthropological Papers, no. 22 (Salt Lake City).

SCHWARTZ, DOUGLAS W., RICHARD C. CHAPMAN, AND JANE KEPP
1980 *Archaeology of the Grand Canyon: Unkar Delta,* Grand Canyon Archaeological Series, vol. 2 (Santa Fe: School of American Research Press).

SCHWARTZ, DOUGLAS W., MICHAEL P. MARSHALL, AND JANE KEPP
1979 *Archaeology of the Grand Canyon: The Bright Angel Site,* Grand Canyon Archaeological Series, vol. 1 (Santa Fe: School of American Research Press).

SELLERS, WILLIAM D. (ED.)
1960 *Arizona Climate* (Tucson: University of Arizona Press).

STACY, HAROLD S.
1970 "Vegetation Studies, Walhalla Plateau," unpublished report on file at the School of American Research, Santa Fe.

THORNTON, GERALD
1969 "Ecological Setting," unpublished report on file at the School of American Research, Santa Fe.

TROTTER, M., AND G. C. GLESER
1958 "A Reevaluation of Estimation of Stature Based on Measurements of Stature Taken During Life and Long Bones After Death," *American Journal of Physical Anthropology* New Series 16:79–124.

WEST, GEORGE
1923 "Cliff Dwellings and Pueblos in the Grand Canyon, Arizona," *Yearbook of the Public Museum of the City of Milwaukee* 3:74–97.